Table of Contents

Introduction

Historically, the United States military has had difficulty articulating and justifying force requirements to civilian decision makers. Since at least 1975, governmental officials and civilian analysts have consistently criticized the military for inadequate planning and execution.[1] Most recently, the wars in Afghanistan and Iraq reinvigorated the debate over the proper identification of force requirements. In February of 2003, Army Chief of Staff, General Eric Shinseki and Deputy Defense Secretary Paul Wolfowitz publically disagreed on the force requirement for Iraq.[2] Pentagon officials advocated a force size around 100,000 soldiers and argued that size force was adequate to provide security during the occupation of Iraq. However, Shinseki testified to Congress that a force of several hundred thousand would be required.[3] The military's inability to define force requirements became a conspicuous issue in late 2009 when the Obama Administration rejected the Army's statement of force requirements for securing Afghanistan. After receiving the initial assessment of 40,000 additional soldiers, the Administration spent three months conducting its own assessment, and as a result, chose to send only 30,000 additional soldiers.[4] The doctrinal planning tools had again provided force estimates that proved unpersuasive.

---

[1] Joseph F. Ciano, "The Quantified Judgement Model and Historic Ground Combat" (masters thesis, Naval Postgraduate School, 1988), 1. Ciano specifically mentions the Mayaguez Rescue, 1975; Iranian Hostage Rescue, 1980; Beirut Peacekeeping Force, 1982; Grenada, 1983; and the Bekaa Valley Air Raid, 1984. While not exhaustive, this list demonstrates that the problem is not new.

[2] Eric Schmitt, "Pentagon Contradicts General on Iraq Occupation Force's Size," *New York Times,* February 28, 2003. http://www.globalpolicy.org/component/content/article/167/35435.html (accessed on 25 October 2011).

[3] Senate Armed Services Committee, *The Fiscal Year 2004 Defense Budget.* 108th Cong., 1st sess., (Washington, D.C.: Government Printing Office, 25 February 2003). http://web.lexis-nexis.com/congcomp/document?_m=807ecde3cf13d08671dfcc3a066773f2&_docnum=152&wchp=dGLz VzS-zSkSA&_md5=83c580e06650ba8e22c748506014e014 (accessed on 02 February 2012).

[4] Elisabeth Bumiller, et al, "How Obama Came to Plan for 'Surge' in Afghanistan," *New York Times*, December 09, 2009. http://www.nytimes.com/2009/12/06/world/asia/06reconstruct.html?pagewanted=all (accessed on 25 October 2011).

Because Army planners have failed numerous times to provide force estimates acceptable to the President, the question arises, why are the planning methods inadequate and why have they not been improved? Military planning doctrine provides methods for calculating force estimates. The methods are designed to determine force requirements for specific military missions or requirements. When the President rejects the Army's advice on troop requirements, he signals that he does not understand what the forces are going to achieve. The Administration does not understand the planning doctrine for force requirements because the models that underlie doctrine are aggregate models; that is, the models produce a gross estimate of a force requirement, not a detailed list of required tasks and associated forces. Aggregation in models provides simplicity but does not provide an explanation because the details about actual employment lie below the resolution level of the model.[5] Therefore, if the Administration wants to know precisely to what ends the recommended forces will be used, the models cannot tell them. The portion of the military planning process that communicates what units are doing is Course of Action Development. Analyzing combat power requirements is just the first step in Course of Action Development. By itself, it can provide an estimate of shortfalls and capabilities, but it is not a finished course of action with detailed missions to subordinate units. Therefore, if the accuracy and utility of a military force estimate is in question, it follows to ask first the question of whether the method used to provide the estimate was suited for the intended purpose. In other words, was the correct method used, or does Army doctrine lack a method for making sound estimates of forces required?

The United States Army's method for determining force requirements is Combat Power Analysis. Combat power is "the total means of destructive, constructive, and information

---

[5] Operations Research Department, *Aggregated Combat Models* (Monterey CA: Naval Postgraduate School, 2000), 1-2 – 1-5. http://faculty.nps.edu/awashburn/Washburnpu/aggregated.pdf (accessed on 18 August 2011).

capabilities that a military unit or formation can apply at a given time."[6] Army planners analyze

combat power as the first step in developing a course of action[7]. *Field Manual 5-0: The*

Operations Process describes three separate and distinct methods for assessing combat power.

The first method is a Correlation of Forces Model (COFM) that aims to establish a rough estimate

of the combat power ratio between opposing forces.[8] The Army designed this model to assess

opponents using Soviet doctrine and equipment. The doctrine developers last updated the data

that supports this method in 2000.[9] Since the publication of *Student Text 100-3: Battle Book* in

2000, the United States Army has changed its organizational structure and has made major

changes in what constitutes combat power. Additionally, near peer, threat forces abandoned

Soviet doctrine and new hybrid threats have emerged. The COFM is outdated and needs to be

updated or replaced.

The Army's second method for assessing combat power is Relative Combat Power

Analysis (RCPA). This method utilizes the elements of combat power to compare enemy

strengths against friendly weaknesses to identify relative advantages and disadvantages.[10] The

process determines for each element of combat power who has the advantage and identifies

significant factors that inform all courses of action under development. Additionally, these

significant factors provide insight into the tactics and procedures used to maximize available

assets. However, RCPA results stand alone and do not influence the calculation of the COFM.

This means that any advantage accounted for by RCPA techniques and procedures have no effect

---

[6] Headquarters, Department of the Army, *Field Manual 3-0: Operations* (Washington, D,C,: Department of the Army, February 2011), 4-1.

[7] Headquarters, Department of the Army, *Field Manual 5-0: The Operations Process* (Washington, D.C.: Department of the Army, March 2011), B-16.

[8] Ibid., B-15.

[9] United States Army Command and General Staff College, *Student Text 100-3: Battle Book* (Fort Leavenworth, KS: USACGSC, 2000), 10-6 – 10-18. http://elearndesign.org/tlacbeta/ikmeC105_norm1/15/xmedia/ST_100-3.pdf (accessed on 5 September 2011).

[10] *FM 5-0: The Operations Process*, March 2011, B-15.

on the COFM. Therefore, the COFM could potentially overestimate or underestimate the relative combat power.

The third method for assessing combat power requirements is a Troops-to-Task (T2T) analysis that allocates resources to accomplish specified and implied tasks. At a fundamental level, T2T is a measurement of troop density to assigned specified and implied tasks. Doctrine reserves this method for stability and civil support operations.[11] However, restricting T2T to stability operations does not support force assessment in full spectrum operations where offensive, defensive, and stability tasks combine. This is a fundamental theoretical problem. T2T assessment is nothing more than a density calculation. The COFM is an example of a counterforce density calculation. Another example of a counterforce density calculation is the old counterinsurgent to insurgent ratio of 10:1 from the 1960s.[12] Fundamentally, these calculations mean that the Army has "x" number of troops compared the enemy's "y" number. An example of troop to area density is unit frontages. These measure how many troops per unit area or linear distance the Army has compared to the enemy. Soldier to population density calculations measure the number of soldiers per civilian in a population. These calculations are fundamental to counterinsurgency as well as stability operations. Thus, the thesis of this paper is that current Army doctrine does not provide a coherent theoretical method for determining force density requirements in the contemporary operating environment. This lack of coherency leads to Administration confusion. Given the need to determine a force requirement, the question becomes why has Army doctrine neglected this issue, and what is the alternative solution?

Research began by thoroughly evaluating the current doctrinal methods for determining force requirements and the rational for their creation. Army doctrinal publications and research

---

[11] *FM 5-0:The Operations Process*, March 2011, B-16.

[12] James T. Quinlivan, "Force Requirements in Stability Operations," *Parameters,* (Winter 1995): 59-69. http://www.carlisle.army.mil/usawc/Parameters/Articles/1995/quinliv.htm (accessed on 26 December 2011).

papers published by government and civilian agencies defined key terms, the planning need at the time the methods were developed, and the concepts that influenced the development of the various methods. The research established that current requirements for assessing combat power are different from the Cold War. However, the larger historical context showed that the requirements in the contemporary operating environment have similarity to historical eras. A review of Army doctrinal publications and government and civilian research papers describe the operating environment and the change in requirements. The research established why the Army retains each method and the planning needs the models address. Therefore, the models still are useful. Nevertheless, at the same time, changed circumstances and mission requirements indicate their logical and methodical points of failure. There are clearly defined areas of Army doctrine that require improvement to provide better estimates of force requirements. The Army's ultimate objective for improving the discussion is to develop confidence among the decision makers in the recommendations.

Given the shortfalls in current Army methods, the current Army doctrine for estimating force requirements is inadequate. It is inadequate because doctrine developers articulate each method as a distinct and separate process. As distinct processes relegated to specific operational themes, they cannot provide a comprehensive picture of force requirements. Currently, the processes are useful in narrowly defined contexts. The research demonstrates that COFM, RCPA, and T2T have useful applications in influencing and informing decision making related to force requirements. The continuing value of these methods explains why Army doctrine writers have retained these methods despite their shortcomings. Essentially, the Army has failed to update the models to account for unified land operations where "forces simultaneously and continuously combine offensive, defensive, and stability operations through a blend of combined arms maneuver and wide area security."[13] Instead of standalone processes, the Army needs an integrated approach to reflect its integrated operational concept. Thus, current Army planning techniques must be modified to determine force requirements to permit reliable estimates of forces needed to perform combined arms maneuver and wide area security simultaneously.

Correlation of Forces Model

The quest to articulate combat power has always been of utmost importance to military thinkers and leaders. Carl von Clausewitz acknowledged that all things being relatively equal between opponents, "superiority of numbers is the most common element in victory."[14] However, combat power is not just about having more assets than an opponent. B.H. Liddell Hart recognized that. He argued that concentration of force in one area is related to and supported by a dispersion in other areas.[15] So, how does the US Army calculate combat power?

The U.S. Army's oldest doctrinal method for calculating combat power is the Correlation of Forces Model (COFM). That model is a planning tool used by planners to help commanders determine if they have enough assets to close with and defeat the enemy with direct and indirect fires. The latest COFM is a Microsoft Excel workbook last updated by the United States Army Command and General Staff College's Department of Tactics in 1999.[16] As shown in Figure 1, COFM calculations consist of several factors related to computing force ratios.

---

[13] Headquarters, Department of the Army, *Army Doctrine Publication 3-0: Unified Land Operations* (Washington, D.C.: Department of the Army, October 2011), 2-3.

[14] Carl von Clausewitz, *On War*, Ed. and Trans. Michael Howard and Peter Paret (Princeton: Princeton University Press, 1976), 194.

[15] B.H. Liddell Hart, *Strategy*, 2nd ed. (New York: New American Library, 1974), 328.

[16] Department of Tactics, "Force_Ratio_Calculator_4ID_CPSOP" *Microsoft Excel Worksheet* (Fort Leavenworth, KS: USACGSOC, 1999). Advanced Military Studies Program Seminar 1 used this force ratio calculator in August of 2011 to aid in planning a division course of action during a training exercise. The doctrine data listed in the worksheet is based on *Student Text 100-3: Battle Book, 1999*. The last update of ST 100-3 to have a force ratio calculator was the 2000 version.

Force Ratios

Friendly Forces					Enemy Forces				
Number	Strength	Type	F.E.	Total	Number	Strength	Type	F.E.	Total
5	100%	Armor Bn (44 x M1A1)	1.24	6.20	3	75%	Infantry Bn (BMP-3)	0.65	1.46
2	100%	Armor Bn (44 x M1A2)	1.30	2.60	1	75%	Tank Bn (TB 40xT90)	1.06	0.80
1	100%	155(SP) Bn (M109A6, 3x6)(Pa	1.50	1.50	1	75%	2S7 Bn	1.28	0.96
1	100%	Atk Helo Bn (24 x AH-64)	5.00	5.00	1	75%	AT Bn (12 x 2A45 & 6 x AT-5/6	0.35	0.26
	100%					80%			
	100%					80%			
	100%					100%			
	100%					100%			
	100%					100%			
	100%					100%			
Friendly Force Equivalent			15.30		Enemy Force Equivalent			3.48	
Ratio of Friendly to Enemy 4.40:1					Ratio of Enemy to Friendly 0.23:1				
Deliberate Attack 5%		<- Mission -> <- Est. Losses ->			Hasty Defense 85%				

Figure 1: Force Ratio Calculator.[17]

The number category is simply the quantity of units in the row. The strength is a measurement of the health of the unit, currently represented as 100% for friendly forces. Type of unit is just that, what kind of unit is represented in the calculator. The force equivalent, designated by F.E., represents the relative weight of a particular type of unit. The total is produced by multiplying the number times the strength times the force equivalent to get the total combat power. Then, the totals of each row are added for a total combat power value called the Friendly Force or Enemy Force equivalent. The combat power values for enemy and friendly, Red and Blue, forces produce a ratio. Planners then compare the resulting ratio against the historical rule-of-thumb force ratios represented in Figure 2. The 4.4:1 force ratio in Figure 1 of Blue to Red informs the planners that with current assets, Blue can execute any of the mission tasks based on historical values. Conversely, Red has enough forces to delay but not defend from a fortified or prepared position. Yet, a ratio greater than historical norms, called a positive COFM result, does not immediately guarantee success.

---

[17] Department of Tactics, "Force_Ratio_Calculator_4ID_CPSOP." *Microsoft Excel Worksheet.*

Historical minimum planning ratios.		
Friendly mission	*Friendly : Enemy*	*Position*
Delay	1 : 6	
Defend	1 : 3	Prepared or fortified
Defend	1 : 2.5	Hasty
Attack	3 : 1	Prepared or fortified
Attack	2.5 : 1	Hasty
Counterattack	1 : 1	Flank

Figure 2: Historical Force Ratios.[18]

There are several problems with the 1999 COFM model. The most glaring problem is that the smallest unit represented in the statistical tables is a battalion.[19] Computing ratios for company sized elements can be calculated by reducing a battalion's value proportionally. However, this mathematical technique is inherently inaccurate because it discounts the synergistic effects of numerical superiority represented by Lanchester equations or network models. The fact that the method is summative is another problem. This is a problem because it fails to represent the impact of combined arms. Combined arms is "[t]he synchronized and simultaneous application of the elements of combat power to achieve an effect greater than if each element of combat power was used separately or sequentially."[20] Thus, the COFM does not estimate gains in combat power achieved when various types of elements are combined. This means that mathematically all combat elements are interchangeable with each other, and the estimated ratios are probably too low.

Combat units are more than interchangeable parts. For example, infantry units are ideally suited to fight in complex terrain such as urban areas or forests. On the other hand, tank units working alone would have significant challenges in forests and urban areas. Also, while field artillery units have awesome destructive firepower, they have no ability to seize and hold terrain.

---

[18] Department of Tactics, "Force_Ratio_Calculator_4ID_CPSOP" *Microsoft Excel Worksheet.*

[19] Ibid. See Appendix A: COFM Technical Data for an example.

[20] Headquarters, Department of the Army, *Field Manual 3-0: Operations* (Washington, D.C.: Department of the Army, February 2011), Glossary-3.

The ability of the COFM to obscure these significant effects by substitution is a problem for the untrained observer. For example, using data located in Appendix A, an Apache attack helicopter battalion with a F.E. of 5.00 is superior to a light infantry battalion with a F.E. of 0.4. However, what if terrain and mission are added to the equation? Is the attack helicopter battalion really 12.5 times more effective than an infantry battalion in triple canopy jungle when the mission is to seize and hold terrain? The situation obviously depends greatly on the mission assigned and the operational environment.

The COFM also suffers from other flaws in the context of the current operational environment. The foundation for the COFM is the 1997 model of combat power. The model for what constitutes combat power has changed since then. The US Army defined combat power in 1997 as "the effect created by combining the elements of maneuver, firepower, protection, and leadership in combat against the enemy."[21] Since 1997, doctrine writers have updated the definition of combat power. Doctrine now defines combat power by eight elements: leadership, information, mission command, movement and maneuver, intelligence, fires, sustainment, and protection.[22] This means that the COFM does not even provide combat values for a majority of what the Army now defines as units having combat value. So, why does the Army retain the COFM as a planning methodology? A look at the lineage of the COFM provides the answer.

Lanchester Equations

Military commanders have historically attempted to determine the quantity of military forces required to achieve their objectives. These measurements generally revolve around two central themes. The first of these themes is numerical advantage. This is contrasted with the

---

[21] Headquarters, Department of the Army, *Field Manual 101-5: Staff Organization and Operations* (Washington, D.C.: Department of the Army, May 1997), 5-11.

[22] *FM 3-0: Operations,* February 2011, v.

second theme focused on the superior quality of units. The problem is how to model the relative importance of unit quality versus numerical superiority.

United States Army Operations Research swelled in importance during the Vietnam conflict. The Army rapidly expanded its programs to recruit, train, and utilize operations research trained personnel in response to Secretary of Defense Robert McNamara's reliance on operations research techniques.[23] The Army's new interest in analytical techniques manifested itself in 1964. In 1964, Brigadier General William DePuy, the assistant chief of operations to Military Assistance Command Vietnam (MACV) demonstrated the use of combined qualitative and quantitative measures. MACV routinely based their requests for forces to the Joint Chiefs of Staff on how a requested battalion would improve the overall force ratio in Vietnam.[24] Initially, MACV based these ratios on the requirement for a 10:1 ratio of counterinsurgents to insurgents for successful operations.[25] However, MACV abandoned the 10:1 counterinsurgency ratio in favor of a 3:1 ratio established for conventional warfare. They did this because there were insufficient U.S. forces to achieve a 10:1 ratio against a very large Viet Cong force.[26] MACV abandoned the counterinsurgency ratio for a conventional warfare ratio because the counterinsurgency ratio was unattainable. For example, the 1966 troop requirements assumed that each United States (U.S.) Army battalion was equivalent to two South Vietnamese or Viet Cong battalions.[27] Based on assessments of the projected future growth of Viet Cong formations, the MACV staff recommended deploying an additional twenty-four combat battalions.[28]

---

[23] Charles R. Schrader, *History of Operations Research in the United States Army, vol II: 1961-1973* (Washington, D.C.: Department of the Army, 2008), 325.

[24] Graham A. Cosmas, *MACV: The Joint Command in the Years of Escalation, 1962-1967* (Washington, DC: Center for Military History, 2006), 204.

[25] Ibid.

[26] Ibid.

[27] Ibid., 241.

[28] Ibid.

Almost a decade later, General DePuy became the first commander of the newly created United States Army's Training and Doctrine Command. Under his tutelage, the Army published the 1976 version of *FM 100-5: Operations* and championed the use of qualitative data in mainstream Army manuals.[29] The evolution of the U.S. Army's doctrinal combat power models can be traced from this baseline publication.

Despite the late entry of qualitative analysis into mainstream Army manuals, the quest for qualitative and quantitative analysis research began even earlier. In 1914, Frederick William Lanchester published *Aircraft in Warfare: The Dawn of the Fourth Arm* and with it, forever changed how military professionals estimate combat power. Lanchester is famous for his "Lanchester equations" that even today form the backbone for attrition calculations in modern combat simulations.[30] In Chapter V of his book, Lanchester laid out the foundation for a model for both ancient and indirect fire warfare called the Lanchester "linear" equation as well as a model for modern and aimed fire warfare called the Lanchester "N-squared" equation. Essentially, both equations are simple mathematical representations of the military concept of concentration. For Lanchester, "[o]ne of the great questions at the root of all strategy is that of concentration; the concentration of the whole resources of a belligerent on a single purpose or

---

[29] Headquarters, Department of the Army, *Field Manual 100-5: Operations* (Washington, D.C.: Department of the Army, July 1976). A comparison of the 1976 manual to previous versions of FM 100-5: *Operations,* clearly demonstrates the infusion of qualitative and quantitative analysis. Almost every page of the 1976 manual has a chart of some sort describing weapon effects and trends.

[30] Missile Defense Agency, "Mathematical and Heuristic Models of Combat with Examples." Jeffrey Strickland. briefing slides presented at the annual Interservice / Industry Training, Simulation, and Education Conference (2009), 54. http://www.simulation-educators.com/uploads/2/7/7/2/2772366/907_notes_min.pdf (accessed 18 August 2011); Office of the Secretary of Defense. Director of Net Assessment, *An Information Age Combat Model.* Jeffrey R. Cares. Contract TPD-01-C-0023, 30 September 2004. http://www.dodccrp.org/events/9th_ICCRTS/CD/papers/166.pdf (Accessed on 17 August 2011). JANUS, which is the Army's high-resolution ground combat simulation, uses a modified Lanchester Law equation for its attrition function.

object."[31] His equations are his answer to what happens when opponents concentrate their forces and fight.

The principle of mass is the modern version of Lanchester's concentration, and mass is defined as the ability to "[c]oncentrate the effects of combat power at the decisive place and time."[32] Mathematically represented by the "N-squared" equation, mass provides a fighting strength to a force that can be "broadly defined as proportional to the square of its numerical strength multiplied by the effectiveness of its individual units."[33] The measurement of mass for two equivalent forces is mathematically represented by the equation: $Nr^2 = Mb^2$,

> where N is the Red units fighting value
>
> M is Blue units fighting value
>
> r is the number of "red" units
>
> and b is the number of "Blue" units.[34]

This equation provides an estimate of which side will win given specific numbers of combatants and their effectiveness.

The Lanchester equations are critical to understanding the development of mathematical models for combat, especially from the 1960's through today. Even though statistician George Box wrote in 1987 that "all models are wrong, but some are useful," Lanchester equations are useful because they provide reasonable estimates of combat outcomes. Specifically, the three Lanchester equations explain direct fire, indirect fire, and hybrid engagements.[35] Because the

---

[31] Frederick William Lanchester, *Aircraft in Warfare: The Dawn of the Fourth Arm* (London: Constable and CO., 1916), 48.

[32] Headquarters, Department of the Army, *Field Manual 1-02:Operational Terms and Graphics* (Washington, D.C.: Department of the Army, September 2004), 1-121.

[33] Lanchester, 48.

[34] Ibid., 50.

[35] George E. P. Box and Norman Richard Draper, *Empirical Model Building and Response Surfaces.* (New York: Wiley 1987), 424.

estimates fit historical experience, modified Lanchester equations form the basis for attrition

functions in modern combat simulations. Planners use these simulations for force design, force

validation, and combat training. Thus, the lessons learned from these simulations have their

foundation in Lanchester equations.

Lanchester equations also provide insight into the relative worth of qualitative versus

quantitative advantage in combat. The following equation is a derivation of the Lanchester "N-

squared" equation. This equation models who will win a direct fire engagement based on

respective size and overall effectiveness of the opponents. Because it models direct fire

engagements, modelers refer to it as the aimed fire model.[36] The aimed fire model assumes that

combatants can all see each other, and therefore, they can shoot each other. Mathematically the

equation expresses the relationship of increased effectiveness compared to increased overall

numbers. The equation is represented as: $X = \dfrac{(n1P1) \times N1^2}{(n2P2) \times N2^2}$

Where X is equal to the correlation of forces.

N1 is the number of N tanks for side 1 and N2 is the number of tanks for side two.

P1 and P2 are the probability of killing (PK) the opponent.

n1 and n2 represents the maximum rate of fire.

To show the utility of the N-squared equation, the formula above was run 100 times under

changing conditions to investigate the impact of unit effectiveness. The results are represented in

Figure 3. The values of N1 and N2 were held constant to isolate the effects of changing

effectiveness on the resulting force ratio. Blue started with a PK of 10% on the first iteration.

Blue's PK then increased by 10% to 20% for the second iteration. Blue's PK then continues to

---

[36] Operations Research Department. *Aggregated Combat Models* (Monterey CA: Naval
Postgraduate School, 2000), 5-10. http://faculty.nps.edu/awashburn/Washburnpu/aggregated.pdf (accessed
on 18 August 2011); John W. R. Lepingwell. "The Laws of Combat? Lanchester Reexamined,"
International Security 12, no. 1 (1987): 89-134. http://www.jstor.org/stable/2538918 (accessed on 16
August 2011), 93.

increase by 10% for each subsequent iteration to a maximum of 100%. The result is a ten iteration

set with Blue's PK increasing by 10% increments. Meanwhile, for each ten-iteration set, the PK

for Red was held constant. Red starts with a 10% effectiveness score for the first ten iterations.

Red's PK then increased by 10% for a total of 20% during iterations eleven through twenty.

Red's PK continues to increase by 10% until it reaches its maximum of 100% during iterations 91

– 100.[37] The model showed that effectiveness of a unit type does not significantly offset the

advantage of numbers when the opponent is at least 40% effective. In Figure 3, once the threat

force achieved at least a 40% PK, the friendly forces could not achieve a 3:1 advantage even with

a 100% PK. This represents a theoretical effectiveness limit beyond which numbers matter more

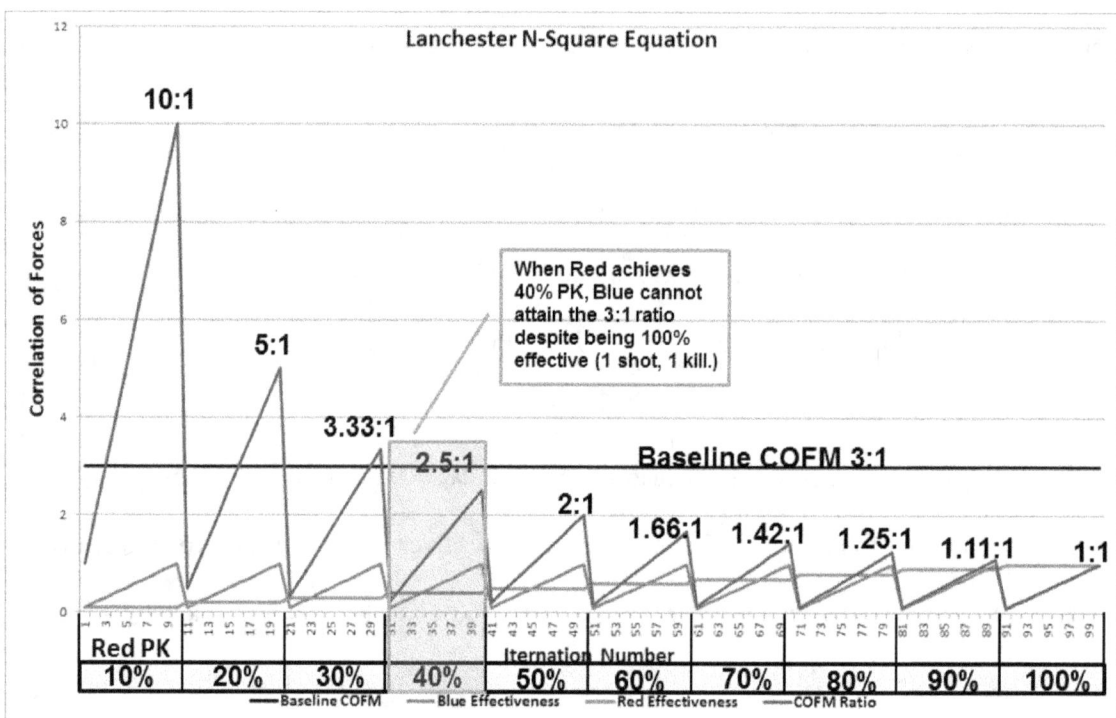

Figure 3: Lanchester N-Square distribution

than overall effectiveness. Yet, if friendly forces use tactics to reduce enemy effectiveness to 30%

PK, then they can attain a 3.33 : 1 ratio. Additionally, if friendly forces can further reduce enemy

---

[37] See Appendix B: Lanchester Equations. Probability of Kill (PK) is used here as a surrogate for total effectiveness in order to simplify the equation and data results.

effectiveness to 20% PK, then the friendly force achieves a 5:1 ratio. These examples represent maximal attainable ratios. However, the data in Appendix B shows that friendly forces actually achieve the minimum 3:1 ratio at less than 100% effectiveness when enemy effectiveness is below 40%.[38] Conversely, when the effectiveness difference between friendly and enemy forces nears 100%, the correlation of forces provides large positive ratios. This means that tactics and technology that grant superior range, target acquisition, and increased lethality provide overwhelming combat power. However, there is a major caveat. Once the enemy negates the range and target acquisition advantage, the enemy effectiveness theoretically approaches the 40% threshold or even exceeds it. Thus, in close combat, the engagement favors the side with superior numbers.

Another important Lanchester equation is the "Linear" equation because it models area fire such as indirect and suppressive fire.[39] The model differs from the "aimed fire" model in its assumption that combatants cannot concentrate their fire on a single target. Therefore, there is no advantage for numbers and the equation weights effectiveness and numbers the same. This means that as effectiveness increases or decreases, it will have a proportionately larger effect than in the "N-square" equation. The "Linear" equation is represented by: $X = \frac{bB}{rR}$

Where X is equal to the correlation of forces.

b and r equal the effectiveness of Blue and Red units respectively.

B and R equal the number of Blue and Red forces opposing each other.

Displayed in Figure 4 below, the "Linear" equation shows a shallower curve compared to the results for the "N-square" equation. This means that Blue forces, under the "N-square" model with a 90% effectiveness compared to Red's 10% effectiveness can achieve a 3:1 ratio when 50 Blue units fight 86 Red units. Under the "Linear" equation, Blue can achieve a 3:1 combat ratio

---

[38] See Appendix B: Lanchester Equations.

[39] Operations Research Department. 5-10.

when 50 Blue units engage 150 Red units. What this law means for planners is that a qualitatively superior Blue force in indirect fire engagements can achieve 3:1 ratios at far lower costs; or rather, smaller Blue units can combat larger units of Red and win in indirect fire.

Combat rarely consist only of indirect fire or aimed fire. Additionally, not all of one side can effectively engage the enemy at a single moment due to terrain restrictions, visibility, distance, or fog of war. Therefore, these models represent maximum theoretical advantages and disadvantages as well as maximum potential combat power. Therefore, modelers use a Lanchester variation called the "mixed combat" model to refine combat results.

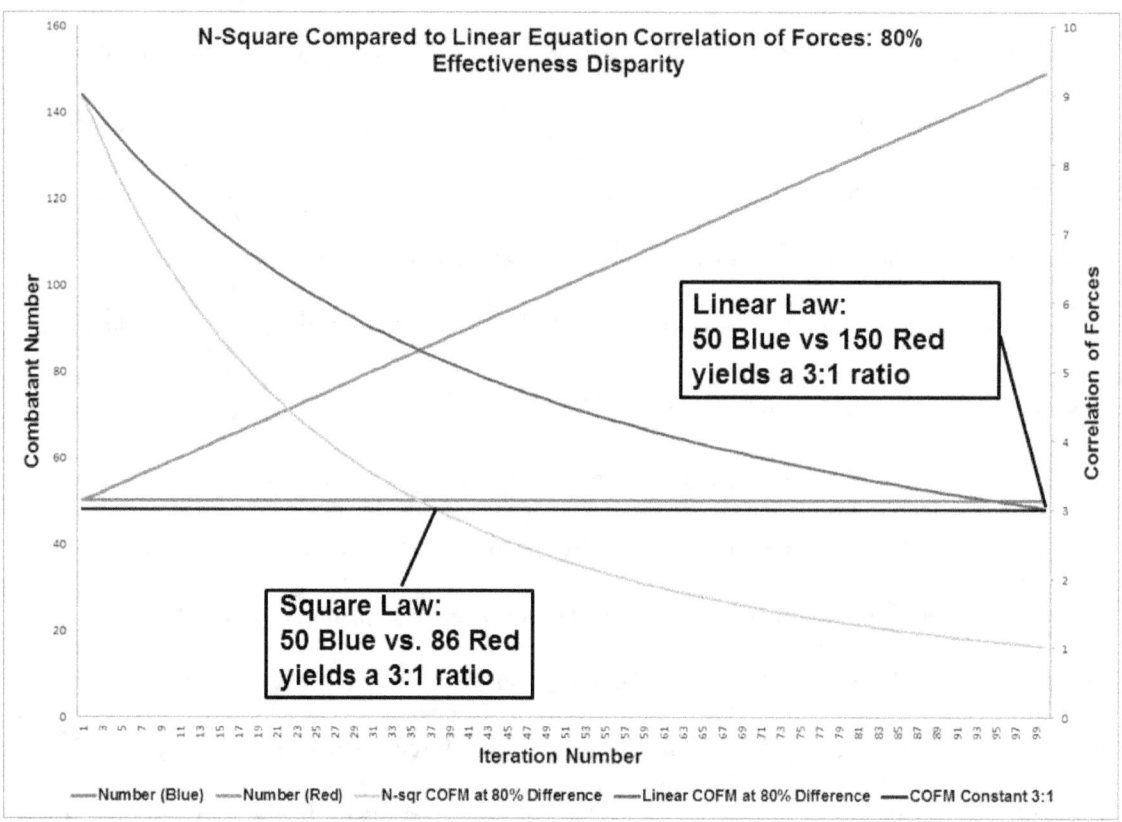

Figure 4: N-Square compared to Linear Law at 80% effectiveness differential.

The mixed combat model, also called the ambush model, blends the two previous equations. In this model, an enemy Red force ambushes a friendly Blue force. The Red force uses aimed, direct fires, so they get the advantage of numbers and concentrated fire under the "N-square" equation.[40] The Blue force is surprised and, therefore, uses area fires and does not benefit

from superior numbers under the Linear Law.[41] The ambush equation is: $X = \frac{bB}{rR^2}$

Where X is the correlation of forces.

b and r equal the effectiveness coefficients for Blue and Red forces.

B and R equal the number of forces present in Blue and Red entities.

This model suggests that a numerically inferior force can successfully ambush a numerically

superior force and achieve a positive correlation of forces. Looking at Figure 5 below, the Red

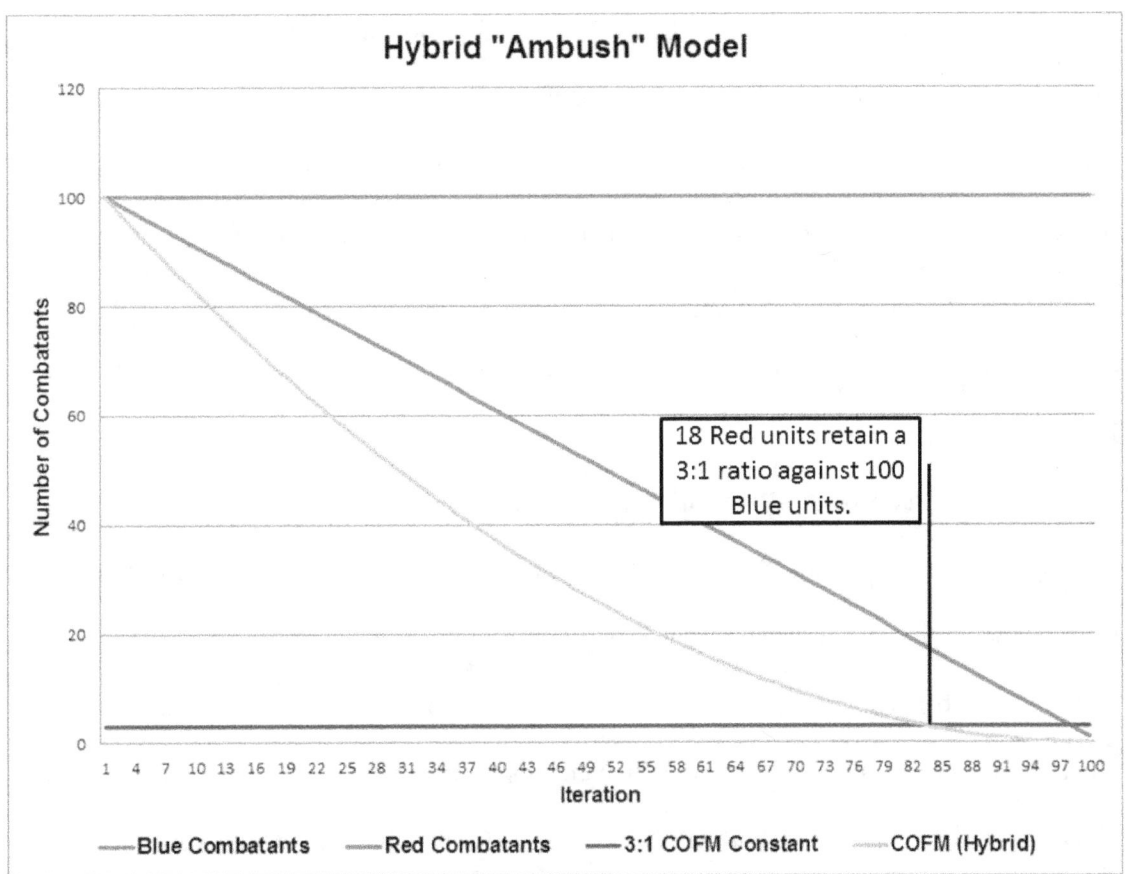

Figure 5: Ambush Model of Combat using Lanchester Equations.

---

[40] Michael J. Artelli and Richard F. Deckro, "Modeling the Lanchester Laws with System Dynamics," *The Journal of Defense Modeling and Simulation: Applications, Methodology, and Technology* 5, no. 1 (2008): 7. http://dms.sagepub.com/content/5/1/1.full.pdf+html (accessed on 16August 2011).

[41] Ibid.

force maintains a 3:1 advantage over Blue until his force strength reaches 17 units compared to Blue's 100. An ambushed, technically superior force no longer benefits from standoff, knowledge superiority, and target acquisition. Most likely, the probability of kill for the Red force is near 100% in an ambush scenario, so the superior effectiveness of Blue is discounted. In reality, Blue's effectiveness would not be 100%, so the data represented in Figure 5 is purposely skewed towards maximal Blue effectiveness. By limiting the changing variable to one entity, the model represents the effect of decreasing numbers of Red forces compared to Blue forces in an ambush scenario. In this particular case, a force of 18 Red combatants achieves a force ratio of over 3:1 against 100 ambushed Blue combatants. The simple logic of the three Lanchester equations remains valid despite being produced almost a century ago.

Network Warfare models validate the inherent logic of Lanchester equations. One of the primary arguments against Lanchester equations is that they represent Industrial Age processes and logic developed almost a century ago. Therefore, they cannot account for networked combat.[42] However, the Lanchester "N-square " equation represents a complete network system in competition against another.

In 2004, Jeffrey Cares' Information Age Combat Model, demonstrated results that approximated Lanchester equation results.[43] Some modelers assumed that effectiveness would be more important in network combat. However, numbers still outweigh effectiveness. Yet, the important number is not the quantity of systems represented in Lanchester equations. The critical number is the number of network nodes combating the enemy.[44] Cares' defines a node in his model as, "one sensor, decider, influencer, and target." Combat between nodes is similar to a Lanchester "N-square" engagement between two like entities. Figure 6 below demonstrates this.

---

[42] Office of the Secretary of Defense, 6.

[43] Ibid.

[44] Ibid., 14.

In Lanchester equations where homogeneous forces fight, such as tank versus tank, a single tank

has sensors, weapons, crew for deciders, and a target they are trying to kill. Thus, Lanchester "N-

square" equations as well as a network models can represent two Blue tanks engaging a single

Red tank. The results will be similar when homogenous combatants are used. This means that

Lanchester equations are still relevant and can describe network engagements on an aggregated

level.

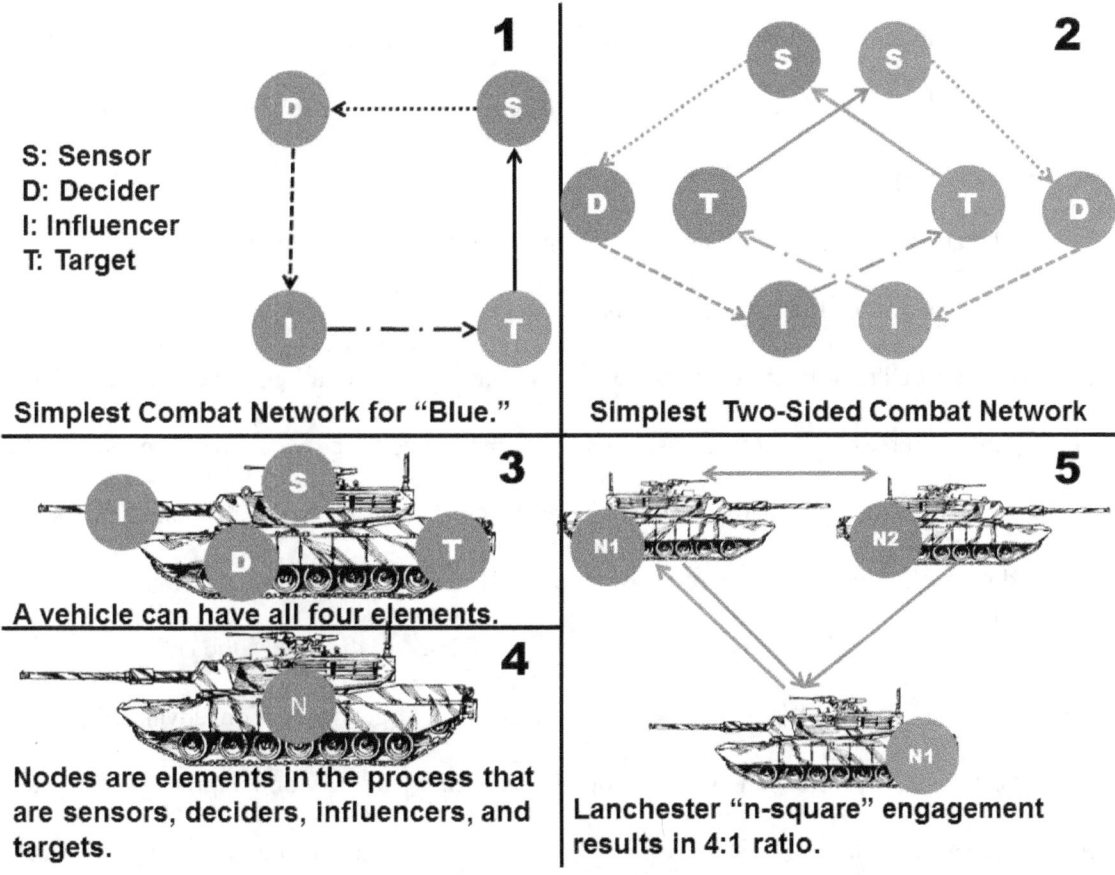

Figure 6: Information Age Combat as Lanchester N-Square Equation.[45]

While the Lanchester equations are informative, they also have some acknowledged

shortcomings. Lanchester equations only account for constant attrition in their relationships.[46]

---

[45] Office of the Secretary of Defense, 7. This is an example of Cares' basic networked combat model. Other networks do exist in which sensors, deciders, influencers, and targets are either independent or combined as a single node. That is why networked combat models only provide approximations of Lanchester equations.

This means that they are unlike real combat where the attrition rate over a given time will fluctuate based on the intensity of the fighting, tactics used by the opponents, and the will of soldiers to survive. Lanchester equations are also static. This means that a modeler assumes a constant style of fire for both sides. In reality, combatants use a mixture of area and direct fires over the course of an engagement. The simple logic of Lanchester equations do not allow or account for movement during battle; they do not account for a side's threshold to sustain casualties before disengaging, surrendering, reinforcing, or fighting harder; and they do not account for target prioritization and allocation.[47] This means that they provide static snap shots of discrete engagements and do not represent dynamic engagements. Therefore, the required ratios are most likely smaller than they should be.

Operationally, the use of Lanchester equations in U.S. Army simulations has led to other problems. The use of the Lanchester "N-Square" equation as a foundation for attrition in simulations can lead to military forces achieving extreme force correlations. Friendly forces achieve extreme force correlations by using tactics to maximize friendly destructive power while minimizing the enemy's destructive power. The results of Lanchester based attrition simulations combined with U.S. operational experiences in the 1991 Gulf War promised a new era in conventional warfare called a Revolution in Military Affairs.[48] In the 1990s, the U.S. Army learned from the first Gulf War that superior weapons range, target acquisition, advanced communications, and precision munitions would allow lighter and networked forces to "see first, decide first, act first, and finish decisively."[49] As a result, U.S. Army acquisition and operational

---

[46] Operations Research Department, 5-10.

[47] Ibid., 5-10.

[48] H. R. McMaster, "On War: Lessons to be Learned," *Survival* 50, no. 1 (2008): 20. http://www.tandfonline.com/doi/pdf/10.1080/00396330801899439 (accessed on 05 September 2011).

[49] Ibid, 21 - 26. Quote is from an AUSA pamphlet that compared Iraq and Afghanistan experiences as consistent with Army transformation. McMaster argues that this is just not the case and is little more than wishful thinking.

approaches assumed combat results due to technological overmatch in line with the extremes of the Lanchester "N-square" equation. Because of this assumption, the Army divested itself of armored formations and increased light and medium forces during transformation. Essentially, the Army risked being lighter and less protected because it could kill the enemy before coming in direct contact.

Contemporary operations such as the wars in Afghanistan and Iraq demonstrate that effectiveness is relative not only to the opponent, but also to the mission, the terrain, and the weather. In Afghanistan, the Tora Bora operation in the Afghan mountains demonstrated how detailed and real time surveillance and precision fires could not "compensate for the lack of ground forces to cover exfiltration routes."[50] This was a failure of effectiveness to compensate for a lack of numbers. During the 2003 Iraq invasion, U.S. V Corps constantly fought battles during movement to contact because enemy forces did not prepare a defensive line and instead intermingled with the population, dispersed, used sandstorms, or used deception to mask their forces.[51] Real operations showed the fallacy of the U.S. Army's assumption that it could avoid contact with an enemy at a time and place of its choosing. Because of the inherent problems with using Lanchester equations in previous wars, the U.S. Army developed the Weapon Effectiveness Index / Weighted Unit Value model.[52]

---

[50] H. R. McMaster, 22.

[51] Ibid.

[52] William J. Krondak, et al., "Unit Combat Power (and Beyond)." paper presented at the annual meeting of the International Symposium on Military Operational Research (ISMOR), (Cranfield, UK, August 2007), 9. http://ismor.cds.cranfield.ac.uk/ISMOR/2008/KrondackCunninghametal.pdf (accessed on 17 August 2011).

Weapon Effectiveness Index, Weighted Unit Value, and Armored Division Equivalents.

The Center for Army Analysis developed the Weapon Effectiveness Index / Weighted Unit Value model in the early 1970s "to provide a gross static measure of a force's combat potential to inform defense acquisition and force structure decisions."[53] In its most basic form, the model indexed the combat units of the North Atlantic Treaty Organization and the Warsaw Pact to a base line unit called the Armored Division Equivalent.[54] Unlike pure Lanchester equations that could only compare like systems to like systems, the Weapon Effectiveness Index / Weighted Unit Value model allowed comparisons between heterogeneous units indexed to a commonly understood baseline. This system enabled comparisons between Soviet block and NATO units.

The ability to compare units of various sizes fielded with assorted weapon systems provided a great advantage over static Lanchester equations or simple numerical comparisons between friendly and threat weapon systems. The model was simple. Essentially, modelers classified every conventional weapon based on functional parameters. The modelers then assessed the individual weapons based on certain technical characteristics shared by the family of weapons. The technical assessments allowed subject matter experts to rank the weapons within categories and thus develop a Weapon Effectiveness Index.

The Weapon Effectiveness Index is the foundation for the Weighted Unit Value and Armored Division Equivalent models. To develop the Weapon Effectiveness Index, modelers classified conventional weapons into nine different categories. The modelers used a Delphi technique to assign each category a weight score. In this particular instance, 109 field grade officers across NATO were surveyed to develop a collective judgment of the worth of systems

---

[53] Krondak, 9.

[54] William P. Mako, *U.S. Ground Forces and the Defense of Central Europe* (Washington, D.C.: The Brookings Institution, 1983), 106.

relative to each other in various terrain.[55] The modelers then used a representative system for the category index. For example, the M60A1 tank was chosen as the base tank for the index of that category of weapon system. Modelers then assessed each different weapon against the category index on their respective firepower, mobility, and survivability to generate index scores.[56] The Weapon Effectiveness Index formula is: $WEI = c_f F + c_m M + c_s S$

> Where WEI is the Weapon Effectiveness Index.
>
> c_x = weighting coefficients of each index.
>
> F = firepower index.
>
> M = mobility index.
>
> S = survivability index.[57]

Modelers computed each factor index with the following equation: Index = $\sum_{i=1}^{n} Q_i C_i$

> Where Q_i = quality scale of the engineering characteristics with a value range
>
> between 1 and 0.
>
> C_i = the weighting factor for the value of the characteristic relative to the others.
>
> n = the total number of characteristic considered in evaluating a weapon system.[58]

Similar to the categories, military experts used a Delphi technique to determine the Weapon Effectiveness Index weighting coefficients.[59] Once the index was established, the modelers used it to generate an aggregate unit score called the Weighted Unit Value.

---

[55] Allen D. Raymond, "Assessing Combat Power: A Methodology for Tactical Battle Staffs" (masters thesis, School for Advanced Military Studies, USACGSC, 1993), 14.

[56] Barry O'Neill, "How to Measure Military Worth (At Least in Theory)." YCISS Working Paper #7 (York Center for International and Strategic Studies: York University, April 1991), 7. http://www.yorku.ca/yciss/publications/WP07-O'Neill.pdf (accessed on 5 September 2011); Krondak, "Unit Combat Power (and Beyond)." 9.

[57] Krondak, "Unit combat Power (and Beyond)," 9.

[58] Ibid., 10.

[59] Ibid.

The Weighted Unit Value is the basis for the Armored Division Equivalent. The Center

for Army Analysis modified this model at least three times during the period from 1974 until

1988 with corresponding names as WUV I, II, and III.[60] To generate the Weighted Unit Value for

a particular unit, the following equation was used: $WUV = \sum_{a=1}^{X}(CW)_a \left[\sum_{n=1}^{y} C_n(WEI)_a\right]$

Where WUV = the Weighted Unit Value for a particular unit.

C_n = the number of combat effective weapons systems of a specific type.

$(WEI)_n$ = weapon effectiveness index for a given weapon system.

$(CW)_a$ = category weight of a given weapon system.

a = integer representing the weapon category (1- ∞).

n = integer representing the types of weapons.

m = total number of weapon types within a weapon category

x = total number of categories of weapons to be accounted for (1-9).[61]

In the case of an U.S. armored division in 1983, the Weighted Unit Value score was 47,490. That

number then became the index number for one Armored Division Equivalent. Planners could now

compare conventional forces in spite of diverse and heterogeneous weapons mixes. The following

diagram shows the values used to calculate the Armored Division Equivalent. Using the

technique outlined above, modelers were able to compare the static combat potential of NATO

and WARSAW pact armed forces. However, despite the seeming scientific rigor of this method,

there were some fundamental flaws in the methodology.

---

[60] O'Neill, "How to measure Military Worth," 7.

[61] Krondak, "Unit combat Power (and Beyond)," 10.

The Weapon Effectiveness Index / Weighted Unit Value / Armored Division Equivalent

model is currently out of favor with the U.S. Army and has been since the late 1980s.[63] The

model primarily suffers from three major drawbacks. First, there is subjectivity built into the

model.[64] Despite the use of a Delphi process to eliminate subjective bias in determining weapon

and criteria weights, subjective judgments provide the foundation for the model. The overall

analysis is subject to compounding judgment errors because the model rests on subjective

judgments for weapon ranking and category weights. The model is also additive. Additivity in

this model means that weapons are interchangeable with no combined arms synergistic effects

---

[63] Krondak, "Unit combat Power (and Beyond)," 11.

[64] Ibid., 10; O'Neill. "How to measure Military Worth," 7.

computed. So, a purely infantry formation can theoretically overcome an armored division if it is large enough.

One final note on Weapon Effectiveness Index / Weighted Unit Value / Armored Division Equivalent models needs to be made. The *CGSC ST 100-3: Battle Book* model discussed above is a permutation of the Weapon Effectiveness Index / Weighted Unit Value / Armored Division Equivalent model. Units are indexed to a Bradley Infantry Fighting Vehicle battalion. It is also interesting to note that the Command and General Staff College (CGSC) published the CGSC model in ST 100-3 and taught the model during calendar year 2000. That is at least a decade after this model fell out of favor with force modelers. Additionally, the 1994 *FM 34-130: Intelligence Preparation of the Battlefield* reinforced the techniques taught at CGSC. Appendix B of FM 34-130 describes combat power assessment using a Weapon Effectiveness Index / Weighted Unit Value methodology indexed to U.S. unit equivalents for combat power analysis.[65] The 1994 method of calculating combat power was the doctrinally prescribed method for intelligence officers and battle staffs until 2009 when the new Army *FM 2-01.3: Intelligence Preparation of the Battlefield* manual deleted this methodology.[66] Therefore, COFM methodology using the tools described above were the doctrinal methods for Operation Enduring Freedom and Iraqi Freedom. Thus, this model provided the foundation for Army force requirements to defeat Iraqi conventional forces, but it could not account for the insurgency that followed.

---

[65] Headquarters, Department of the Army, *Field Manual 34-130: Intelligence Preparation of the Battlefield* (Washington, D.C.: Department of the Army, 1994), B-38.

[66] Headquarters, Department of the Army, *Field Manual 2-01.3: Intelligence Preparation of the Battlefield* (Washington, D.C.: Department of the Army, October 2009), 4-1 – 4-9. The conventional COFM methodology is no longer found in the new field manual and has been replaced by a lot of Counter Insurgency and stability operations language. The technical appendices from the old manual that describe frontage tables, force arrays, and methods for calculating combat power are totally removed. Intelligence specialists are directed to reference database materials for threat arrays.

Historical Ratios

Until now, historical ratios, exemplified by the 3:1 ratio of forces required for a successful attack, have been treated as fact. In accordance with conventional practice, a friendly force that achieves the established ratio guidelines is able to execute its wartime tasks: 3:1to attack a prepared position; 2.5:1 to conduct a hasty attack; 1:1 counterattack; 1:2.5 execute a hasty defense; 1:3 defend from prepared position; and 1:6 delay.[67] These rules of thumb are important because they establish a statistical baseline for successful operations. Essentially, if a force achieves a historical force ratio, then the U.S. Army states that it historically has a 50% chance of success.[68] The overriding question then becomes, what is measured to determine the force ratio? If doctrine articulates a requirement for 3:1 for a successful attack, what is being measured?

This question is not new. Joshua Epstein asked this question in his 1988 article in *International Security* titled "Dynamic Analysis and the Conventional Balance in Europe."[69] His argument against accepting historical ratios consisted of three parts. First, advocates for the ratios needed to specify clearly what units were being compared in the historical data.[70] Second, the units chosen must be present for a scientifically valid section of the historical record. Third, once the first two were accomplished, the statistical data resulting from the comparison must support the ratios advocated.[71] Based on Epstein's research using a U.S. Army Concepts Analysis Agency database of over 601 battles, the attacker succeeded with less than a 3:1 ratio in 59% of the

---

[67] Headquarters, Department of the Army, *Field Manual 5-0: The Operations Process* (Washington, D.C.: Department of the Army, March 2010), B-16.

[68] Ibid.

[69] Joshua M. Epstein, "The 3:1 Rule, the Adaptive Dynamic Model, and the Future of Security Studies," *International Security* 13, no. 4 (1989): 90 - 91. http://www.jstor.org/stable/2538781 (accessed on 16 August 2011).

[70] Ibid., 91.

[71] Epstein, 91.

represented battles.[72] Statistically, this does not equate to the U.S. Army's assertion in the 2010 version of *FM 5-0: The Operations Process* that a unit with a historical ratio has a 50% chance of success. The doctrine is 9% more conservative and will possibly lead to an over estimation of the forces required for success.

However, John Mearsheimer disputed Epstein's findings in the same issue of *International Security* in his article, "Assessing the Conventional Balance: The 3:1 Rule and its Critics." Mearsheimer provides what he calls empirical evidence. First, he says that the 3:1 rule has to be valid because military experts across broad nationalities and military experience all agree that concentration at a weak point on the order of 3:1 is a principle of war.[73] He gives a historical basis for the rule originating in Europe between the Franco Prussian War of 1870 - 71 and World War I.[74] He argues that the Prussians, French, and other European great powers determined through their own historical analysis of wartime experience that this rule was valid.[75] However, Mearsheimer's best evidence was drawn from the work of General William E. DePuy and the doctrinal changes in the Army during the 1970s. Mearsheimer cited a General Depuy article from the April 1979 edition of *Army* magazine in which the 3:1 rule was said to have been validated by US Army Training and Doctrine Command using war games and analysis conducted by the Combined Arms Center at Fort Leavenworth.[76] Mearsheimer concluded that there is plenty of evidentiary support for the 3:1 rule, but it has not been proved by a scientific survey of historical data.[77]

---

[72] Epstein, 106.

[73] John J. Mearsheimer, "Assessing the Conventional Balance: The 3:1 Rule and Its Critics," *International Security* 13, no. 4 (1989): 59. http://www.jstor.org/stable/2538780 (accessed on 16 August 2011).

[74] Ibid.

[75] Ibid., 60.

[76] Ibid.

[77] Ibid., 62.

Therefore, how does one reconcile Epstein's use of the CAA database to refute or at least place the 3:1 rule in question? Looking at a copy of the CAA database report reveals that there are numerous factual inconsistencies within the database.[78] Four external reviewing agencies identified data inconsistencies during the quality assurance check of the data. The U.S. Army's Military History Institute, The Center for Military History, the History Department at West Point, and the Combat Studies Institute commented that there were problems of data source validity for constructing the database.[79] Databases for statistical analysis are only as good as the data they contain. Unfortunately, processing historical records for six hundred and one battles across four centuries proved impractical for the CAA study. Thus, Epstein's use of the CAA data does not prove or disprove the 3:1 rule because his research was based on questionable data. Therefore, a planner should be wary of using the Army practice of historical ratios with their associated 50% chance of success rate. Additionally, there is still the unanswered question of what is measured when military professionals say they need a 3:1 advantage to attack. Based on the identified problems, is correlation of forces methodology useful?

Correlation of Forces methodology is still relevant and valid for conventional forces in today's contemporary operating environment. The Weapon Effectiveness Index and Weighted Unit Value methods in particular provide interesting possibilities. Hybrid threat forces can be assessed and assigned combat power equivalents based on standard indexing methods. It does not matter what entities are compared. Units can be indexed. However, the major problem is the sheer volume of intelligence collection and analysis resources that would need to be committed to index hybrid forces. In the past, the U.S. Army had years to compare Soviet forces to its own. The

---

[78] US Army Concepts Analysis Agency, "Analysis of Factors that have Influenced Outcomes of Battles and Wars: A Data Base of Battles and Engagements," vol 1 Main Report, Trevor N. Dupuy (September 1984), B-I-3. http://www.dtic.mil/dtic/tr/fulltext/u2/b086797.pdf (accessed on 19 December 2011).

[79] US Army Concepts Analysis Agency, 2-1 - 2-2.

situation in the future is likely different. Threats will consist of conventional forces, irregular forces, criminal organizations, and terrorists groups working together. The sheer volume of potential threats will force prioritizing the elements of hybrid forces to be indexed. A comprehensive combat power comparison beyond a few defined configurations is unlikely. The question is then, to what level does the U.S. Army resolve its index?

In the past battalions were the largest formations in the doctrinal models. Battalions are not the answer in the contemporary operating environment. For friendly forces, the ability to model smaller and smaller combat entities is necessary. In the current environment platoons operate independently, which means there is a need to model below the platoon level. There is nothing theoretically preventing the Army from indexing the combat power of a company, platoon, squad, fire team, or crew. However, not all Army companies, platoons, squads, teams, and crews are created equal. An updated weapon index and weighted unit index that accounts for smaller units would therefore be beneficial.

Additionally, future research must improve the old method of indexing. An updated model must consider the new model of combat power based on the War Fighting Functions. Firepower, survivability, and maneuverability, the basis of the old Weapon Effectiveness Index/ Weighted Unit Value/Armored Division Equivalents model, no longer comprises the entirety of combat power. Fires, information, intelligence, etc. must have at least a multiplying effect in the combat power calculation. If not, the models will continue to be theoretically different from the doctrine they supposedly support. The difference between published theory and practical application will continue to confuse decision makers and, thus, raise doubts about the recommended force requirements. Additionally, current COFMs cannot model the effect of tactics and morale on the result of engagements and battles. These morale factors are traditionally ignored by modelers in equations because they are extremely difficult to quantify and replicate. However, the Army developed a planning tool to correct this shortfall within the COFM. This planning tool is called Relative Combat Power Analysis.

Relative Combat Power Analysis

Relative Combat Power Analysis (RCPA) is an essential tool for planners and commanders. This tool provides a link between the art and science of war. The COFM is an attempt to use quantitative analysis in determining force requirements for resolving military problems. RCPA on the other hand specifically enables planners and the commander to utilize the art of war to better estimate the combat power of not only their own forces, but also the enemy. Planners designed RCPA specifically to incorporate what are historically called moral factors. RCPA is relatively new since it entered Army doctrine with the 2005 version of FM 5-0.[80] The only example the Army provided for RCPA in its manuals is located in the 2005 version of *FM 5-0: Army Planning and Orders Production*. Figure 8 below is a copy of the RCPA example from the 2005 manual. The 2005 model is out of date given the new definition of combat power. Combat power now consists of the six-warfighting functions: Mission Command, Movement and Maneuver, Fires, Sustainment, Intelligence, and Protection multiplied through Information and Leadership. The 2005 example provides no link to force ratio estimates. Despite these problems, it provides planners insightful information.

The outcome of the RCPA model is a series of deductions that planners use to inform the development of courses of action.[81] The deductions generally take the form of tactics, techniques, and procedures that will maximize friendly forces while negating enemy strengths. This is problematic since the deductions that are the output of the model are absent in the 2005 example. The example does show who has an advantage or disadvantage for a given element of combat power. However, without the inferences, the model is useless.

---

[80] A review of the 1997 and 2005 versions of FM 5-0 show that the only method for assessing combat power was the COFM for the 1997 version.

[81] *FM 5-0: The Operations Process,* March 2011, B-15.

Elements of Combat Power	Enemy strengths/ weaknesses	Friendly strengths/ weaknesses	Advantage	
			Friendly	Enemy
MANEUVER	Strength: Infantry with numerous anti-tank weapons. Weakness: Poorly maintained equipment. Lack of mobility between battle positions.	Strength: 3 X M1A2 equip combined arms task forces.	X	
FIREPOWER	Weakness: Limited to mortar fires.	Strength: Air supremacy, unopposed CAS, rocket and cannon fires.	X	
PROTECTION	Strength: Fully constructed defensive position with overhead cover.	Strength: Night vision capability; weapons standoff. Weakness: Soft skin vehicles and dismounted infantry.		X
LEADERSHIP	Strength: Elite unit very disciplined. Weakness: Lack of initiative by subordinates without orders from higher command.	Strength: Combat tested unit. Aggressive and offensive oriented command climate.	X	
INFORMATION	Strength: Full backing of local population and regional press. Weakness: C2 very acceptable to jamming and interception.	Strength: Secure and reliable C2 systems. Weakness: Seen as invaders and occupiers by opposing force and local population.		X

Figure 8: Example of the 2005 FM 5-0 RCPA.[82]

The current FM 5-0 published in 2011 does not improve clarity either. The new FM 5-0 does not

even provide an example. It also fails to identify how planners utilize the deductions in course of

action development. Additionally, the doctrine vaguely states that planners will have insight on

friendly vulnerabilities to protect, friendly advantages to exploit, enemy vulnerabilities to attack,

and enemy strengths to avoid.[83] Furthermore, Army doctrine only vaguely describes the

components of combat power that make up the RCPA model contained in Chapter 4 of *FM 3-0:*

Combat Power (February 2011). The fifteen page chapter provides no method for measuring the

elements of combat power.[84] Therefore, the model depicted in 2005 and revisited in the 2011

version of FM 5-0 is underdeveloped. Any force recommendations resulting from this method are

questionable because the model lacks scientific rigor.

---

[82] Headquarters, Department of the Army, "Figure 3-9," in *Field Manual 5-0: Army Planning and Orders Production* (Washington, D.C.: Department of the Army, January 2005), 3-32.

[83] Ibid.

[84] *FM 3-0:Operations,* February 2011, 4-1 – 4-15.

If the RCPA method is ill defined, the question then becomes, what is the utility of the RCPA and why does the Army list it as a viable planning tool? RCPA ultimately does not result in a mathematical equation or numerical result. What it does provide are critical insights into aspects of military operations not contained within standard COFM assessments. The deductions that result from matching enemy strengths to friendly weakness drive decisions about how to best protect friendly forces and offset enemy strength. Looking at friendly strengths compared to enemy weaknesses allows planners to deduce the tactics, techniques, and procedures required to defeat the enemy efficiently. It also allows planners to maximize combat potential to offset numerical inferiorities. Ultimately, this method is about using the art of war to defeat the enemy. As art it cannot be readily quantified into total numbers of assets required to win. Yet, like a painting by a master artist, you have to have elements of all warfighting functions to create a masterpiece. Therefore, applying the model to a hypothetical situation best demonstrates the utility of the method.

Figure 9 is an updated RCPA that incorporates the latest doctrine. What the reader will immediately notice is that the model now includes two critical components missing from the last published version in 2005. The six-warfighting functions are listed and a designated space for deductions is included. When the movement and maneuver and fires sections from the RCPA model are applied, the friendly forces are assessed to have an advantage in movement across the battlefield. The enemy will most likely defend from prepared positions in restrictive terrain to offset the friendly advantage in armor and movement. The enemy can utilize urban areas or other restrictive terrain to force friendly units to close the distance and, thus, lose the standoff advantage. However, friendly forces have a limited number of precision guided munitions

33

Element of Combat Power	Friendly	Enemy	Advantage		Deductions
			Friendly	Enemy	
Movement and Maneuver	Strengths: - 2x Combined Arms Battalions - 1x Armored Reconnaissance Squadron - Average movement speed of units is 20kph - Average endurance of formations is 200 kilometers	Strengths: - 2x Light Infantry battalions with numerous ATGM systems in complex terrain. -1x Partisan company	X		1) Friendly forces can use superior mobility to engage the enemy at time and place of choosing. 2) The Enemy can only defend from restrictive terrain in order to maximize his forces. 3) Surprise will be difficult to achieve with our large movement signature and partisan presence in our security area.
	Weakness: - large movement signature	Weakness: - limited ability to reposition w/ 3kph movement rate.			
Fires	Strengths: - 1x Fires battalion of 16x 155mm - 2x 120mm MTR platoons - 1x Q-36 Radar - 1x Q-37 Radar - 36x rounds of Excalibur - 2x Attack Weapon Teams	Strengths: - Partisan employment of IEDs - 81mm and 60mm Mortars	X		1) Friendly weight of fires can decisively determine the outcome of any engagement where collateral damage is not a major factor. 2) Relatively limited assets for precision engagement require strike ROE and CDE. 3) Enemy assets will co-locate in protected areas and engage US forces. 4) The information threshold will need to be increased to allow the attack of legitimate targets once a site's protected status is violated by the enemy.
	Weakness: - Weight of fires is non precision - CDE will decrease responsiveness	Weakness: - no integrated fire command			

Figure 9: Example of a RCPA. For the Full RCPA see Appendix C.

that they can use to assist in driving the enemy from restrictive terrain. Additionally, since the enemy will use urban terrain, friendly forces can use information operations to condition the battlefield for lethal operations. Friendly forces will do this by communicating to all audiences about the locations and identities of structures deemed protected such as religious, cultural, essential services, and educational. Friendly forces will communicate that if the enemy violates the protected status of designated buildings, the buildings can be destroyed out of military necessity. Friendly forces will also communicate their intentions to the civilian populous to help drive a wedge between them and the enemy forces. As demonstrated, this narrative provides insight to the interaction of friendly and enemy combat forces.

Again, the RCPA does not produce quantitative results. What it does provide is a narrative of reasonable expectations about the nature of the operation being planned. It appears as if RCPA is not integrated with the COFM for force assessment. In reality, they are integrated but only incidentally. If a planner knows he needs a capability based on deductions resulting from the RCPA, he requests the capability from the higher headquarters. The narrative generated from producing the RCPA is the most valuable part. It is valuable because RCPA has the ability to transcend hard numbers and provide an insight into how forces are used. This tool has powerful explanatory value for decision makers before a course of action is developed.

RCPA currently does not provide a direct input to the COFM. Planners should be able to use the identified advantages or disadvantages to provide the basis for adjustments to the COFM. In the particular case presented in this paper, the friendly force held the advantage in five of the six-warfighting functions. However, there are no metrics established in the literature. Without these metrics, a planner is just making subjective assessments on what effect the advantages or disadvantages have on the force. Finally, RCPA does not readily assist planners in determining force requirements for stability operations. RCPA provides insights into how forces can execute stability operations, but it does not provide a hard force requirement number. Therefore, the Army established Troops-to-Task analysis to offset this problem.

Troops-to-Task Assessment

Troops-to-task (T2T) analysis is the Army's newest method of determining force requirements for stability or civil support operations. The model made its first appearance in the 2008 version of FM 5-0.[85] Defined in *FM 5-0: The Operations Process* (March 2011), T2T analysis compares available resources to specified or implied tasks.[86] T2T analysis specifically "provides insight as to what options are available and whether or not more resources are required."[87] One of the primary techniques for assessing T2T requirements specifically in counterinsurgency operations is troop to population density.[88] The Army recommends minimum troop densities that fall within the range of 20 – 25 counterinsurgents per 1000 members of the

---

[85] A comparison of the 1997 and 2005 versions of FM 5-0 with the 2008 version demonstrate this fact.

[86] *FM 5-0: The Operations Process,* March 2011, B-16.

[87] Ibid.

[88] Ibid., B-17.

population.[89] Despite these recommendations, the Army also states that no fixed troop density guarantees success in counterinsurgency. The Army also utilizes a second method for conducting T2T analysis. This method is clearly outlined in *FM 3-24.2: Tactics in Counterinsurgency*. The method is depicted in Figure 10 below. The first step is similar to conducting

		AO Platoon Requirements				
		AO 1	AO 2	AO 3	AO 4	AO 5
Specified or Implied Tasks	Secure key infrastructure	3	2	3	1	
	Establish and secure CMOC					2
	Conduct population control	3	3	4	3	
	Conduct route security					3
	Conduct base security (COPs)	1	1	1	0	1
	Secure PRT					1
	Totals:	7	6	8	4	6

Steps:
1. Subdivide urban areas into AOs based on demographics.
2. List specified and implied tasks.
3. Determine a combat power metric such as 1 x PLT per key infrastructure, or 2 x PLT to secure the CMOC.
4. Fill out table with number of platoons, and tally at bottom to determine how many platoons are required for each AO.
5. Consolidate AOs if possible, and assign HQ.

Figure 10: Example Troops-to-Task Assessment using platoon sized elements.[90]

a COFM assessment. Planners must determine what size element is going to be the baseline for the assessment. In this case, a platoon is the recommended entity. The planners then list out the specified and implied tasks that a unit must execute to be successful. Since the Army doctrinally reserves troops-to-task assessments for stability operations, tasks are focused more on wide area security as compared to combined arms maneuver tasks. Once the task requirements are

---

[89] *FM 5-0: The Operations Process,* March 2011, B-17; Headquarters, Department of the Army, *Field Manual 3-24: Counterinsurgency* (Washington, D.C. : December 2006), 1-13.

[90] Headquarters, Department of the Army, *Field Manual 3-24.2: Tactics in Counterinsurgency* (Washington, D.C.: Department of the Army, March 2009), 3-15.

determined, the planner is then able to assess if his unit has the internal capacity to accomplish the missions. If the unit does not have the internal capacity, it must request additional assets from the higher headquarters, reprioritize missions, or assume risk.

The T2T model found in Army doctrine has some fundamental flaws that are not evident in the doctrinal material. The T2T model has the same defect as the COFM model. Regardless of the type of unit chosen as the indexing entity, there is always the problem that not all Army units are equal. In the case of battalion sized elements, the maneuver battalions of the Infantry Brigade Combat Team (IBCT) at the small unit level differ radically from the elements of the Heavy Brigade Combat Team and the Stryker Brigade Combat Team (SBCT). Figure 11 and Appendix D depict these differences. For the purpose of this discussion, only combat formations at the platoon, section, and squad level are included. Additionally, only the primary maneuver fighting formations are compared. Missing from this comparison are the Brigade Reconnaissance, Fires, Troops, and Support battalions.

Differences in Combat Platoon Strength Across Maneuver Battalion and Combat Platoon Types						
	Brigade Combat Team Type	Infantry Brigade Combat Team		Stryker Brigade Combat Team		Heavy Brigade Combat Team	
	Maneuver Battalion Type	Infantry Battalion		Stryker Infantry Battalion		Combined Arms Battalion	
		Total Platoons	Soldiers per Platoon	Total Platoons	Soldiers per Platoon	Total Platoons	Soldiers per Platoon
Platoon Type	Tank	0	0	0	0	6	16
	Infantry	9	39	12	45	6	42
	Scout	1	18	1	21	1	24
	Mortar	1	24	1	27	1	26
	Weapons	4	14	0	0	0	0
	Mobile Gun System	0	0	3	9	0	0

Figure 11: Shows the differences between U.S. Army Combat Platoons.[91]

Based on the above figure, what size platoon does a planner use to index his platoon requirements? In the Combined Arms Battalion, a planner has six infantry platoons of forty-two men; six tank platoons of sixteen men; one scout platoon of twenty-four men; and one twenty-six man mortar platoon. Therefore, if the planner chooses a tank platoon of sixteen soldiers as the

---

[91] Product is of the authors own creation using Army Field Manuals. See Appendix D: U.S. Army Brigade Combat teams and their Combat Platoons.

indexing requirement to fulfill the troops-to-task, he has to figure out the number of sixteen man platoons his companies can field. Each tank company will be able to field three sixteen-man platoons. Each infantry company can field seven sixteen-man platoons with fourteen soldiers uncommitted. The battalion mortar platoon at twenty-six men and the battalion scout platoon at twenty-four men can cross-level and field three, sixteen man platoons for the Headquarters and Headquarters Company. The Combined Arms Battalion would then have the ability to internally support twenty-three, sixteen man platoon requirements. By comparison, the Stryker Infantry battalion can support thirty-five platoons of sixteen men while the Infantry Battalion can support twenty-eight platoons of sixteen men. As this example demonstrates, determining force requirements based on the number of platoons required depends on what kinds of platoons are available based on the units employed. Platoons are not equal in the army inventory.

Any articulation of the troops-to-task methodology that indexes platoons has a major flaw. To generate the twenty-three platoons of sixteen men across the Combined Arms Battalion, established crews and squads must be broken up. Soldiers will be cross-leveled to other organizations, sometimes out of the company, to achieve the proper manning levels. Established leadership chains are broken and new ones are constructed ad hoc. Furthermore, the cross leveling of certified crews and squads impacts a unit's readiness. Thus, the ability of the Combined Arms Battalion to reorganize for combat is degraded.

In addition to the indexing method for determining troops-to-task requirements for stability operations, there is another method called troop density. Troop density is calculated in three ways. Troop density is calculated by determining the number of soldiers within a given unit area; the number of soldiers relative to the enemy; and the number of soldiers relative to the population. Troop density calculations that compare friendly forces relative to enemy forces are exemplified by the COFM, historical ratios, and counterinsurgency calculations that assume a ratio of ten counterinsurgents to one insurgent. Troop density as a function of geographic area is generally represented by unit frontages. Troop density relative to population is the measurement used for estimating force requirements in population centric counterinsurgency operations. However, only calculations of troop density relative to the population are represented explicitly in Army doctrine.

The calculation of troop density per volume of terrain is one of the oldest methods of calculating force requirements. An example of how this model is used is the conventional force calculations between Soviet and NATO forces stationed in Europe during the Cold War. One of the planning assumptions included in the calculation was that a division could defend no more than a twenty-five kilometer front.[92] Therefore, to defend the seven-hundred and fifty kilometer Central Front, NATO needed thirty divisions.[93] Additional considerations increased the required number of divisions. If NATO intended to hold at least a third of its divisions in reserve, the requirement increased to forty-five divisions.[94] Also, if NATO intended to maintain its stated objective of establishing a relative force ratio of 1.5:1, it needed a total of "fifty-three divisions to counter an enemy force equivalent to eighty divisions."[95] NATO did not possess that many divisions.

The planning factor in 1983 was the Armored Division. The division contained eighteen thousand, three-hundred men.[96] Therefore, the division manpower equivalent was the number of men in the armored division. Based on the above planning scenarios, the following troop numbers were required: 549,000 men for thirty divisions, 825,500 men for forty-five divisions, and 969,900 men for fifty-three divisions. In 1983, NATO maintained roughly twenty-one manpower division equivalents.[97] Obviously, that number was well short of the stated alliance goals.

---

[92] Mako, 39.

[93] Ibid.

[94] Ibid.

[95] Ibid.

[96] Ibid.

[97] Ibid., 49.

Currently, troops per unit area calculations are not in vogue in the U.S. Army. The current series of manuals do not mention recommended unit frontages.[98] This is most likely an acknowledgement that when used at a macro level, unit frontages were unpersuasive to decision makers. As shown above, when NATO determined they needed fifty-three divisions, the political leaders determined that the cost was too high. They never fielded the manpower and hedged their bets with a doctrine predicated on the use of tactical nuclear weapons.

A second method for calculating force density for counterinsurgency operations focused on a force requirement comparison of the number of counterinsurgents to the insurgents. Generally known as the 10:1 ratio of counterinsurgents to insurgents, planners advocated this ratio in Malaya and Vietnam.[99] However, the ratio was questioned at the time because of fundamental problems with assumptions in the methodology.[100] Despite the problems, the methodology reemerged during the Reagan Administration. The Administration assumed that ten or more counterinsurgents were needed to tie down one insurgent. Therefore, policy advocates insisted that the United States could contest the Soviet Union in Afghanistan by expending resources at a ratio of 1:10. The US Government could do this cheaply by supporting Afghan rebels to bleed the Soviet Union.[101] Despite the seeming success of the Reagan Administration's approach, the U.S. Army definitively discounts this methodology in the 2006 edition of *FM 3-24: Counterinsurgency.*[102]

---

[98] A review of the field manuals used to build Appendix D resulted in no mention of unit frontages. The manuals are referenced in Appendix D in the footnotes for each combat battalion type.

[99] James T. Quinlivan, "Force Requirements in Stability Operations," *Parameters,* (Winter 1995): 59-69. http://www.carlisle.army.mil/usawc/Parameters/Articles/1995/quinliv.htm (accessed on 26 December 2011).

[100] Ibid.

[101] Joshua Thiel, "COIN Manpower Ratios: Debunking the 10 to 1 Ratio and Surges," *Small Wars Journal* (January 2011), http://smallwarsjournal.com/jrnl/art/coin-manpower-ratios-debunking-the-10-to-1-ratio-and-surges (accessed on 6 September 2011).

[102] *FM 3-24: Counterinsurgency,* 1-13.

The Army discounts the 10:1 ratio of counterinsurgents to insurgents for the same reasons identified in during the Vietnam War. The major problem is how can a planner or analyst determine the actual number of insurgents. The nature of guerillas or insurgents is such that they blend in with the population. They are not easily distinguished. Additionally, a planner cannot account for members of the population that exhibit "Accidental Guerilla" tendencies as described in David Kilcullen's 2009 book *The Accidental Guerilla*. The accidental guerilla is a member of the local populous who fights as part of a backlash to foreign intervention as opposed to real ideological commitment. The answer to more successful analysis lies in the third method of articulating force requirements.

The best method of articulating force requirements in counterinsurgency operations is a troop density comparison as a function of the population within the area of operations. This method is the method advocated in the US Army counterinsurgency manual.[103] Despite general academic agreement that population based ratios are the most promising way for determining force requirements. Military analysts disagree about the ratio required to successfully prosecute a counterinsurgency or stability operation. The disagreement centers on what is the requirement for counterinsurgent forces. One of the largest areas for criticism and disagreement between the military and civilian policy makers is the number of troops required for successful operations. This disagreement is also present within the ranks of the military community. The public debate between General Stanley McChrystal and members of the Obama Administration over the number of soldiers required to secure Afghanistan is emblematic. The question boils down to how someone can say there were too many or not enough troops for any given operation. Three years before the debate, the U.S. Army counterinsurgency manual provided a baseline index value in 2006. The manual urged a minimum ratio of 20 - 25 counterinsurgents for every 1000 members

---

[103] *FM 3-24: Counterinsurgency*, 1-13.

of the population.[104] However, the validity of that statement is questioned by contemporary and recent scholarship. So, where did the ratio come from?

John J. McGrath, a researcher for the US Army's Combat Studies Institute, published *Boots on the Ground: Troop Density in Contingency Operations* in 2006. That was the same year the counterinsurgency manual was published. McGrath's study pointed out that the counterinsurgency manual numbers are based on the 1995 and 2003 work of James T. Quinlivan.[105] So, to understand why Quinlivan generated the numbers used in the Army counterinsurgency manual, it was necessary to look at his original work. Quinlivan published "Force Requirements in Stability Operations" in the Winter 1995 edition of *Parameters*. Quinlivan, at the time was the director of the Arroyo Center at RAND.[106] He published the article as part of the debate over the U.S. Army's post-Cold War roles and missions. His specific contribution was the fundamental shift in logic from an enemy focused requirement to a population based requirement. His specific rational was, "the purpose of stability operations--to create an environment orderly enough that most routine civil functions could be carried out--suggests that the number of troops required is determined by the size of populations."[107] Quinlivan again added to the debate by publishing "The Burden of Victory: The Painful Arithmetic of Stability Operations" in the *RAND Review* in the summer of 2003. It is here that he claimed that force sizes of 20 troops to 1000 members of the population are required for success. The basis for his claims is an analysis of British experience in over twenty-five years stabilizing

---

[104] *FM 3-24:Counterinsurgency*, 1-13.

[105] John J. McGrath, *Boots on the Ground: Troop Density in Contingency Operations* (Fort Leavenworth, KS: Combat Studies Institute Press, 2006), 1.

[106] Quinlivan, "Force Requirements in Stability Operations."

[107] Ibid.

Northern Ireland as well as NATO experiences in Bosnia and Kosovo.[108] Based on the need for twenty troops per one thousand population members, Iraq would need five-hundred-thousand troops for stabilization. However, the problem with Quinlivan's claim and the U.S. Army's use of 20 troops to 1000 members of the population is that the historical sample was too small, consisting of only six operations: Somalia, Haiti, Bosnia, Kosovo, Iraq, and Afghanistan.

John J. McGrath suggested that a security force density of 13.26 troops per 1000 member of the population is adequate and better supported by historical analysis.[109] McGrath used the term security forces because he included police functions as part of stabilization requirements. He based his estimate of police force requirements on large American cities and their police departments: New York, Chicago, Philadelphia, Boston and Los Angeles. His average of 4.1 police officers per 1000 population is a result. Therefore, among the 13.26 troops required for stability, 4.1 have to perform police duties, or roughly 31% of the total force.[110] McGrath's study has problems similar to Quinlivan's study. It uses a relatively small number of case studies. He used the Philippines 1901, Post World War II Germany, Post War Japan, Malaya, Bosnia, Kosovo, and Iraq.[111] However, unlike Quinlivan's study of two decades, McGrath's work covers a century of contingency operations. The increased historical scope potentially provides a broader perspective of historical norms as compared to two decades.

Steven M. Goode, added to force requirement debate in 2009 with his article "A Historical Basis of Force Requirements in Counterinsurgency." Goode shed new light on the topic because he had access to the Center for Army Analysis (CAA) Irregular Warfare Database. So, unlike McGrath and Quinlivan, who between themselves looked at fifteen total cases studies

---

[108] James T. Quinlivan, "Burden of Victory: The Painful Arithmetic of Stability Operations" *Rand Review* (Summer 2003). http://www.rand.org/publications/randreview/issues/summer2003/burden.html (accessed on 25 December 2011).

[109] McGrath, 147-148.

[110] Ibid.

[111] Ibid., vi – ix.

for force requirements, Goode could assess over one-hundred conflicts.[112] CAA's purpose in developing the database was an attempt to place the force levels in Afghanistan and Iraq into historical perspective.[113] However, to do that the CAA needed to clearly distinguish counterinsurgency from Quinlivan's stability operations and McGrath's contingency operations. First, the Irregular Warfare Database was sorted by localizing all of the conflicts that matched the counterinsurgency definition.[114] Second, those cases where a third party's conventional forces were involved, such as Vietnam, were excluded. This left forty-two cases that matched the definition. The analysis solely focused on force levels and not on the other aspects of counterinsurgency, such as tactics and operational approaches. What researchers found was that not only does the population determine the force requirement needed, but the force requirement was also dependent on the level of violence. The following equation resulted from the study. This equation gives a threshold for minimum troop level to decrease violence in counterinsurgency operations. $F = 1.2 \times \left(\frac{K}{L}\right)^{0.45} + 2.8$ where:

F = security forces required per 1,000 population to reduce violence

K = number of security forces killed annually, per million population

L = fraction of security forces local to the conflict.[115]

Using the equation above, Goode reported that 89% of the time three observations were made. The first observation was that violence reduced when counterinsurgent forces achieved the threshold force level or exceeded it. The second observation was that violence increased until the

---

[112] Steven M. Goode, "A Historical Basis for Force Requirements in Counterinsurgency," *Parameters* (Winter 2009-10), 47.

[113] Ibid., 48.

[114] Goode, 48. Insurgency defined as: an organized movement aimed at the overthrow of a constituted government through use of subversion and armed conflict. Counterinsurgency defined as: those military, paramilitary, political, economic, psychological, and civic actions taken by a government to defeat insurgency.

[115] Ibid., 53.

insurgents won in cases where the counterinsurgents did not achieve the threshold force level. Finally, if the counterinsurgent forces contained no local security forces, they failed.[116] Goode had one additional conclusion. Violence would increase or decrease in a coming year based on the current force level. However, the change in the level of violence only occurred 69% of the time. Goode also used the above equation to determine the threshold of security forces in Afghanistan for the winter of 2009. Using a population figure of 28.9 million and a reported violence figure of fifty killed in action for every million inhabitants, and a local security force that is 65% of the overall security force in country, the required number of security forces is a ratio of 11:1000.[117] Goode's threshold is two higher than the reported nine security forces per one thousand on the ground. Thus, based on Goode's research, the mission in Afghanistan would experience increasing levels of violence until a force level of 11:1000 was achieved. Thus, the increase in killed in action in Afghanistan from 521 in 2009 to 711 in 2010 may be attributable to insufficient forces.[118]

The Institute for Defense Analysis (IDA) refined the study of troop densities even more in March of 2010. They published a report titled *Force Sizing for Stability Operations.* That study also used the Center for Army Analysis Irregular Warfare (CAA IW) Database. Despite the report's title, the analysts used counterinsurgencies, not stability operations, as a worst case planning assumption.[119] IDA used forty-one of the CAA IW database case studies that matched counterinsurgency criteria. They modified the database data to compare troop densities based on actual population within an area of operation as opposed to the database standard of using a

---

[116] Goode, 53.

[117] Ibid., 54.

[118] iCasualties.org, "Operation Enduring Freedom," iCasualties.org, http://icasualties.org/OEF/ByYear.aspx (accessed on 04 February 2012).

[119] Institute for Defense Analysis, *Force Sizing for Stability Operations,* R. Royce Kneece Jr., et. al., IDA Paper P-4556, (March 2010), http://dodreports.com/pdf/ada520942.pdf (accessed on 06 October 2011), iii.

country's total population.[120] What IDA determined was that a force density of 16:1000 in the actual area of military operations resulted in a 50% probability of success. The data also showed that a force density of 40:1000 resulted in a 75% chance of success.[121] Based on this statistical analysis, the IDA researchers concluded that the 20:1000 minimum ratio advocated by Quinlivan and articulated in the 2006 Counterinsurgency manual was validated. What was not validated was the upper range of 25:1000. Conflicts in certain cases had far higher ratios of about 30 – 50 counterinsurgents per 1000 members of the population.[122] What is crucial about this study is that it shows that there is a significant relationship between force density and avoidance of defeat.[123] Planners and policy decision makers would be highly interested in a finding that informed them that without a certain counterinsurgent density, the probability of success falls below a significant threshold. For example, a policy maker could decide that he wants a troop cap on the total number of deployed troops. This threshold now allows planners to advise decision makers on what a troop cap would mean for chances of success. So, if a decision maker wants at least a 50% chance of success based on troop commitment, the army will need to achieve a total force density of 20:1000. Using a hypothetical population of 6 million persons, the bill in total counterinsurgents would be 120,000 security forces. If a policy maker sets the force strength cap at 60,000, then there is a 60,000 security force shortfall. Also, the chance of success falls to around 42% based on IDA's research.[124] Therefore, at least 60,000 more counterinsurgents need to be fielded.

---

[120] Institute for Defense Analysis, iv; Center for Army Analysis, "Irregular Warfare." Database 2011. The CAA database gives measurement for total population within an entire country. The researchers had to modify the data by subtracting populations and areas determined to not be within the actual zone of conflict.

[121] Institute for Defense Analysis, 6.

[122] Ibid., 2.

[123] Ibid., 10.

[124] Ibid., 6.

However, the existing doctrine on force requirements does not benefit from recent research. The Troops-to-Task model, currently found in *FM 5-0: The Operations Process* is ill conceived. Restricting its usage to just stability operations is a falsehood. Under the heading of troops-to-task falls the calculation of troop commitments based on some measure of density. For major combat operations, the troops-to-task method of choice is a COFM model and historical force ratios that compare combatants to each other. Troops-to-Task can also be a measure of troop density to a specific area of operation as demonstrated in the Cold War frontage calculations. Additionally, Troops-to-Task may just be a measure of troop density to specified and implied tasks. The utility of the Troops-to-Task model for stability and counterinsurgency is well established. However, the methodology articulated in doctrine to perform the analysis is lacking. There is no reason that a planner should have to dig through two layers of field manuals down into *FM 3-24.2: Tactics in Counterinsurgency* to find the first clear articulation of a Troops- to-Task methodology. Additionally, the existing doctrinal discussion on troops-to-task is severely limited. Recent research now provides the Army with new tools to reinvigorate the discussion of troops-to- task calculations. Goode's calculation that relates troop requirements to violence levels and a minimum of host nation security is one such tool. Additionally, the IDA analysis determined that certain force levels provide a statistically significant probability of not failing. That is another useful insight.

Conclusion.

Army planners have continually failed to persuade decision makers to accept recommended force requirements. So, why were the planning methods inadequate and why have they not been improved? Research showed that the three models used by Army doctrine to estimate force requirements comprise a small sample of the available historical models and contemporary advanced models developed through new research techniques. The models reviewed in this paper were the Correlation of Forces Model, Lanchester equations, Weapon

Effectiveness Index / Weighted Unit Value / Armored Division Equivalent, Historical Force

Ratios, Relative Combat Power Analysis, Troops-to-Task density, Unit Frontages, and Troops to

Population density. Each model was shown to have its own appropriate application.

Correlation of Forces models are the oldest methods for calculating combat power. As

such, they have the most research behind them. The COFM was adequate for comparing U.S.

forces to Soviet equipped formations. However, threats have evolved beyond Soviet doctrine

since the COFM was last updated. The current operating environment requires models that

account for hybrid threats containing elements of conventional, irregular, criminal, and terrorist

components. Another shortcoming of the COFM is its failure to permit estimates for units smaller

than battalions in military operational environments in which platoons and squads are critical.

Hence, COFM is not useful in the contemporary operating environment.

Like the COFM, Lanchester equations are adequate to model homogeneous system on

system engagements and explain the value of numerical superiority as compared to qualitative

superiority in high intensity combat. As such, modelers use them in some form to drive attrition

functions in combat simulations. Lanchester equations also explain networked combat when

forces are maximally connected. However, Lanchester equations fail to account for

heterogeneous force engagements such as combined arms and conventional versus irregular

forces engagements. Thus, the value of Lanchester models is currently limited.

Weapon Effectiveness Index/Weighted Unit Value/Armored Division Equivalent

methods do allow planners to model combat between dissimilar combatants. The indexing

methodology allowed modelers to index any number of threat and friendly combatant forces.

Unfortunately, the model is additive and cannot not explain the role of increased numerical or

qualitative superiority. In addition, the model depends on identifying the number and type of

weapon systems resident in a combatant and does not account for morale, leadership, and

training. Additionally, historical force ratios have not been empirically validated. While there is wide spread agreement on their use as a rule of thumb, no one knows what military capabilities the ratio actually represents.

The Relative Combat Power Analysis model is the weakest of the three Army doctrinal models. There is little to no academic work on the RCPA model. Yet, RCPA offers promise as the sole means of blending the art and science of war into a combat power calculation. RCPA considers tactics, techniques, and procedures, considerations useful to planners during course of action development. It also illuminates capability shortfalls. However, RCPA provides no evidence upon which to base an estimate for numerical force requirements. The COFM and the T2T assessments are quantitative assessments. The RCPA is a subjective qualitative assessment. At its heart, the RCPA remains the commander's and staff's tool by which to define their best military judgment. For that reason, the analysis RCPA provides will always be subject to criticism.

The final method considered was the Troop-to-Task model. The Troops-to-Task model has a solid historical basis. This is despite the fact it was only published recently. Troops-to-Task methodology is nothing more than the identification of a force density required for mission success. COFM is actually and older version of Troop-to-Task. Older versions used unit frontages to define troop-to-task densities. These methods are well established despite the criticism leveled against them. However, this model suffers from the fact that it is currently ignored and has been removed from military doctrine. Therefore, a planner has no immediate tool with which to determine how long a front a U.S. brigade can defend. The newest version of troops-to-task density is just now achieving maturity. Troop-to-task density calculations based on specified and implied tasks provide an answer to how many of a given sized unit are required for a mission. The major problem with this model is that it is relies on employing standard size units. U.S. Army units do not have standard sizes despite similar designations.

The most recent addition to Army doctrine for force requirements is the definition of troop to population density. The method provides a gross force estimate for counterinsurgency and stability operations. The latest research points to improved methods for assessing force requirements not accounted for in Army doctrine. These methods should be included in Army discussions of combat power assessments.

Considering the limitations of Army force planning methods, it is fair to conclude that Army force estimates have failed to persuade civilian decision-makers because the advice is not supported by a consistent valid method for estimating the force requirements. The models the Army used to calculate combat power have not kept pace with the Army's new capstone doctrine and they do not address full spectrum operations. The current tools are tied to an operational theory in which defense, offense, and stability operations occur at discrete moments and not simultaneously. The three methods for estimating force requirements currently found in Army doctrine may provide a basis for developing a more relevant system to support full spectrum operations. However, the research here could not determine how that might be accomplished. What is clear is that the current methods have utility when dealing with military situations that mirror the conditions represented by each model. In the contemporary military operating environment, the doctrinal models no longer fit.

Appendix A: COFM Technical Data

Friendly		Enemy	
Type	Force Equivalent	Type	Force Equivalent
Infantry Bn (58 x M113)	0.71	Infantry Bn (32 x BTR-50 / 60) N	0.29
Infantry Bn (44 x M2)	1.00	Infantry Bn (32 x BTR-70 / 80)	0.36
Infantry Bn (Light)	0.40	Infantry Bn (32 x BMP-1 / 2) N	0.51
Infantry Bn (Airborne/Air Assault)	0.50	Infantry Bn (BMP-3)	0.65
-----		Infantry Bn (Light / Air Assault)	0.35
Armor Bn (44 x M1A1)	1.24	Infantry Bn (Airborne)	0.50
Armor Bn (44 x M1A2)	1.30	-----	
-----		Recon Bn	0.20
Armored Cav Regiment	11.40	AT Bn (12 x 2A45 & 6 x AT-5/6)	0.35
Armored Cav Squadron	2.80	AT Bn (IMiBn / AT Regt)	0.21
R&S Squadron	0.20	-----	
-----		Tank Bn (MIB 40xT55/62) N	0.77
Combined Arms Bn (29xM1, 29xM2, 3xM3)	1.79	Tank Bn (MIB 40xT64 / T72) N	0.89
Armed Recon Sqd (23 x M3, 12 x LRAS)	0.52	Tank Bn (MIB 40xT80)	1.00
SBCT Bn (Stryker x 53)	0.93	Tank Bn (MIB 40xT90)	1.06
-----		Tank Bn (TB 31xT55 / T62) N	0.60
155(T) Bn (M198, 2x6)	0.70	Tank Bn (TB 31xT64 / T72)	0.69
105(T) Bn (M102, 3x6)	0.70	Tank Bn (TB 31xT80)	0.78
105(T) Bn (M119, 3x6)	0.75	Tank Bn (TB 40xT90)	1.06
155(SP) Bn (M109A5, 3x6)	1.20	Indep Tank Bn (51xT55/62) N	0.98
155(SP) Bn (M109A6, 3x6)(Paladin)	1.50	Indep Tank Bn (51xT64 / T72) N	1.13
155(T) Bn (M198, 3x6)	1.05	Indep Tank Bn (51xT80)	1.28
155(SP) Bn (M109A6, 2x8) (PALADIN)	1.33	Indep Tank Bn (51xT90)	1.36
105(T) Bn (M119, 2x8)	0.67	-----	
MLRS Bn (M270A2, 3x6)	4.50	2A36 Bn	0.75
ATACMS Bn (B2)	6.00	2A65 Bn	0.75
ATACMS Bn (B1)	10.00	2S1 Bn	0.90
-----		2S3 Bn	1.05
Div Cav Sqdn (AASLT Div) (32 x OH-58D)	4.10	2S5 Bn	1.13
Div Cav Squadron (Abn Div) (24 x OH-58D)	3.10	2S7 Bn	1.28
Div Cav Squadron (Lt Div) (16 x OH-58D)	2.10	2S9 Bn	0.60

Figure 12: COFM Technical Force Equivalent Data.[125]

---

[125] Department of Tactics, "Force_Ratio_Calculator_4ID_CPSOP" *Microsoft Excel Worksheet.* (Fort Leavenworth, KS: USACGSOC, 1999).

Div Cav Squadron (Heavy Div) (16 x OH-58D)	3.80	2S19 Bn	1.35
-----		2S23 Bn	0.60
Atk Helo Bn (24 x OH-58D)	3.00	9A51 Bn	3.78
Atk Helo Bn (24 x AH-64)	5.00	9A52 Bn	3.60
-----		BM 21 Bn	3.15
Armoured IN BN (UK Challenger/Warrior)	1.29	BM 21V Bn	1.04
Armoured IN BN (UK Warrior/Challenger)	1.49	BM 22 Bn	3.50
Recce Regt (UK BN)	0.45	BM 24 Bn	1.60
Mechanized IN BN (UK MASTIFF 2)	0.86	D20 Bn	0.68
-----		D30 Bn	0.60
Mechanized BN (ACV-300)	1.10	FROG Bn	0.22
Tank BN (Leo 1A3)	1.15	M46 Bn	0.68
		M240 Bn	4.20
		SCUD Bn	8.40
		SCUD-B Bn	4.20
		SS-21 Bn	6.30

		Hind- D Bn (40) N	3.30
		Hind-E Bn (40)	4.17
		HOKUM / HAVOK Bn (40)	5.83
		Tank Bn (TB 40xT100)	1.06

Figure 13: COFM Technical Force Equivalent Data[126]

[126] Department of Tactics, "Force_Ratio_Calculator_4ID_CPSOP" *Microsoft Excel Worksheet.* (Fort Leavenworth, KS: USACGSOC, 1999).

Appendix B: Lanchester Equations

Run	P (Blue)	P (Red)	N(Blue)	N(Red)	r(Blue)	r(Red)	COFM
1	0.1	0.1	10	10	1	1	1
2	0.2	0.1	10	10	1	1	2
3	0.3	0.1	10	10	1	1	3
4	0.4	0.1	10	10	1	1	4
5	0.5	0.1	10	10	1	1	5
6	0.6	0.1	10	10	1	1	6
7	0.7	0.1	10	10	1	1	7
8	0.8	0.1	10	10	1	1	8
9	0.9	0.1	10	10	1	1	9
10	1	0.1	10	10	1	1	10
11	0.1	0.2	10	10	1	1	0.5
12	0.2	0.2	10	10	1	1	1
13	0.3	0.2	10	10	1	1	1.5
14	0.4	0.2	10	10	1	1	2
15	0.5	0.2	10	10	1	1	2.5
16	0.6	0.2	10	10	1	1	3
17	0.7	0.2	10	10	1	1	3.5
18	0.8	0.2	10	10	1	1	4
19	0.9	0.2	10	10	1	1	4.5
20	1	0.2	10	10	1	1	5
21	0.1	0.3	10	10	1	1	0.333333
22	0.2	0.3	10	10	1	1	0.666667
23	0.3	0.3	10	10	1	1	1
24	0.4	0.3	10	10	1	1	1.333333
25	0.5	0.3	10	10	1	1	1.666667
26	0.6	0.3	10	10	1	1	2
27	0.7	0.3	10	10	1	1	2.333333
28	0.8	0.3	10	10	1	1	2.666667
29	0.9	0.3	10	10	1	1	3
30	1	0.3	10	10	1	1	3.333333
31	0.1	0.4	10	10	1	1	0.25
32	0.2	0.4	10	10	1	1	0.5
33	0.3	0.4	10	10	1	1	0.75
34	0.4	0.4	10	10	1	1	1
35	0.5	0.4	10	10	1	1	1.25
36	0.6	0.4	10	10	1	1	1.5
37	0.7	0.4	10	10	1	1	1.75
38	0.8	0.4	10	10	1	1	2
39	0.9	0.4	10	10	1	1	2.25
40	1	0.4	10	10	1	1	2.5
41	0.1	0.5	10	10	1	1	0.2
42	0.2	0.5	10	10	1	1	0.4
43	0.3	0.5	10	10	1	1	0.6
44	0.4	0.5	10	10	1	1	0.8
45	0.5	0.5	10	10	1	1	1
46	0.6	0.5	10	10	1	1	1.2
47	0.7	0.5	10	10	1	1	1.4
48	0.8	0.5	10	10	1	1	1.6
49	0.9	0.5	10	10	1	1	1.8

50	1	0.5	10	10	1	1	2
51	0.1	0.6	10	10	1	1	0.166667
52	0.2	0.6	10	10	1	1	0.333333
53	0.3	0.6	10	10	1	1	0.5
54	0.4	0.6	10	10	1	1	0.666667
55	0.5	0.6	10	10	1	1	0.833333
56	0.6	0.6	10	10	1	1	1
57	0.7	0.6	10	10	1	1	1.166667
58	0.8	0.6	10	10	1	1	1.333333
59	0.9	0.6	10	10	1	1	1.5
60	1	0.6	10	10	1	1	1.666667
61	0.1	0.7	10	10	1	1	0.142857
62	0.2	0.7	10	10	1	1	0.285714
63	0.3	0.7	10	10	1	1	0.428571
64	0.4	0.7	10	10	1	1	0.571429
65	0.5	0.7	10	10	1	1	0.714286
66	0.6	0.7	10	10	1	1	0.857143
67	0.7	0.7	10	10	1	1	1
68	0.8	0.7	10	10	1	1	1.142857
69	0.9	0.7	10	10	1	1	1.285714
70	1	0.7	10	10	1	1	1.428571
71	0.1	0.8	10	10	1	1	0.125
72	0.2	0.8	10	10	1	1	0.25
73	0.3	0.8	10	10	1	1	0.375
74	0.4	0.8	10	10	1	1	0.5
75	0.5	0.8	10	10	1	1	0.625
76	0.6	0.8	10	10	1	1	0.75
77	0.7	0.8	10	10	1	1	0.875
78	0.8	0.8	10	10	1	1	1
79	0.9	0.8	10	10	1	1	1.125
80	1	0.8	10	10	1	1	1.25
81	0.1	0.9	10	10	1	1	0.111111
82	0.2	0.9	10	10	1	1	0.222222
83	0.3	0.9	10	10	1	1	0.333333
84	0.4	0.9	10	10	1	1	0.444444
85	0.5	0.9	10	10	1	1	0.555556
86	0.6	0.9	10	10	1	1	0.666667
87	0.7	0.9	10	10	1	1	0.777778
88	0.8	0.9	10	10	1	1	0.888889
89	0.9	0.9	10	10	1	1	1
90	1	0.9	10	10	1	1	1.111111
91	0.1	1	10	10	1	1	0.1
92	0.2	1	10	10	1	1	0.2
93	0.3	1	10	10	1	1	0.3
94	0.4	1	10	10	1	1	0.4
95	0.5	1	10	10	1	1	0.5
96	0.6	1	10	10	1	1	0.6
97	0.7	1	10	10	1	1	0.7
98	0.8	1	10	10	1	1	0.8
99	0.9	1	10	10	1	1	0.9
100	1	1	10	10	1	1	1

Figure 14: Lanchester Equation Qualitative vs. Quantitative Run

Appendix C: Relative Combat Power Analysis Example

Element of Combat Power	Friendly	Enemy	Advantage Friendly	Advantage Enemy	Deductions
Movement and Maneuver	Strengths: - 2x Combined Arms Battalions - 1x Armored Reconnaissance Squadron - Average movement speed of units is 20kph - Average endurance of formations is 200 kilometers Weakness: - large movement signature	Strengths: - 2x Light Infantry battalions with numerous ATGM systems in complex terrain. -1x Partisan company Weakness: - limited ability to reposition w/ 3kph movement rate.	X		1) Friendly forces can use superior mobility to engage the enemy at time and place of choosing. 2) The Enemy can only defend from restrictive terrain in order to maximize his forces. 3) Surprise will be difficult to achieve with our large movement signature and partisan presence in our security area.
Fires	Strengths: - 1x Fires battalion of 16x 155mm - 2x 120mm MTR platoons - 1x Q-36 Radar - 1x Q-37 Radar - 36x rounds of Excalibur - 2x Attack Weapon Teams Weakness: - Weight of fires is non precision - CDE will decrease responsiveness	Strengths: - Partisan employment of IEDs - 81mm and 60mm Mortars Weakness: - no integrated fire command	X		1) Friendly weight of fires can decisively determine the outcome of any engagement where collateral damage is not a major factor. 2) Relatively limited assets for precision engagement require strike ROE and CDE. 3) Enemy assets will co-locate in protected areas and engage US forces. 4) The information threshold will need to be increased to allow the attack of legitimate targets once a site's protected status is violated by the enemy.
Sustainment	Strengths: - 4x Forward support companies -1x BSB Weakness: Logistical assets require roads to transport bulk fuel.	Strengths: - Relatively light sustainment footprint - Sustainment flow from national and partisan sources Weakness: - LOCs are subject to interdiction fires (surface and air) - Partisan support is a double edged sword in that the populous will only support the enemy living off the land so long as it does not threaten their survival	X		1) Cutting the enemy LOC to support their conventional forces will be relatively ineffective so long as the partisan company is able to facilitate resupply. 2) Neutralization of the partisan company as well as attacking the LOCs will isolate the enemy. 3) Sustainment assets represent our weakest area and will need augmentation for protection.
Intelligence	Strengths: - Superior technical intelligence - UAVs Weakness: - HUMINT undeveloped	Strengths: - prevalence of HUMINT Weakness: - limited to no national Intel support	NA	NA	1) Our superior technical intelligence will enable us to attack enemy conventional forces freely. 2) Our lack of HUMINT makes targeting the partisan company extremely difficult.
Protection	Strengths: - Armored unit - Soldier PPE is state of the art - CREW systems - standoff capability of weapons Weakness: - equality of forces at short ranges - easily identifiable due to uniforms	Strengths: - light forces and partisans are able to blend into complex terrain - prepared defensive positions - HUMINT allows advanced warning Weakness: - lack of robust ADA - lack of counter fire radars - no armored protection for soldiers or systems - limited medical support	X		1) critical to the operation is using all means to separate combatants from the population. Inform and influence activities will shape the environment to mitigate this issue. 2) maximal use of standoff via IDF and aviation is critical to maintaining our combat power
Mission Command	Strengths: - Highly trained NCOs leading small units - Highly trained officer corps - robust command and control system Weakness: - ability to micro manage	Strengths: - Conventional forces are highly trained for combat tasks with competent leadership - small units are disciplined and exercise initiative Weakness: - formation not designed for maneuver warfare - limited command and control architecture	X		1) Because the enemy fights best from fixed positions, efforts should be focused to attack his flanks and rear areas 2) Do not expect enemy units to crack and break. Their junior leaders will enable small units to fight competently when cut off or surrounded 3) we can overwhelm the enemy's limited C2 architecture and cause it to fail.

Figure 15: RCPA example that improves upon the 2005 model.

Appendix D: U.S. Army Brigade Combat Teams and their Combat Platoons.

Infantry Battalion

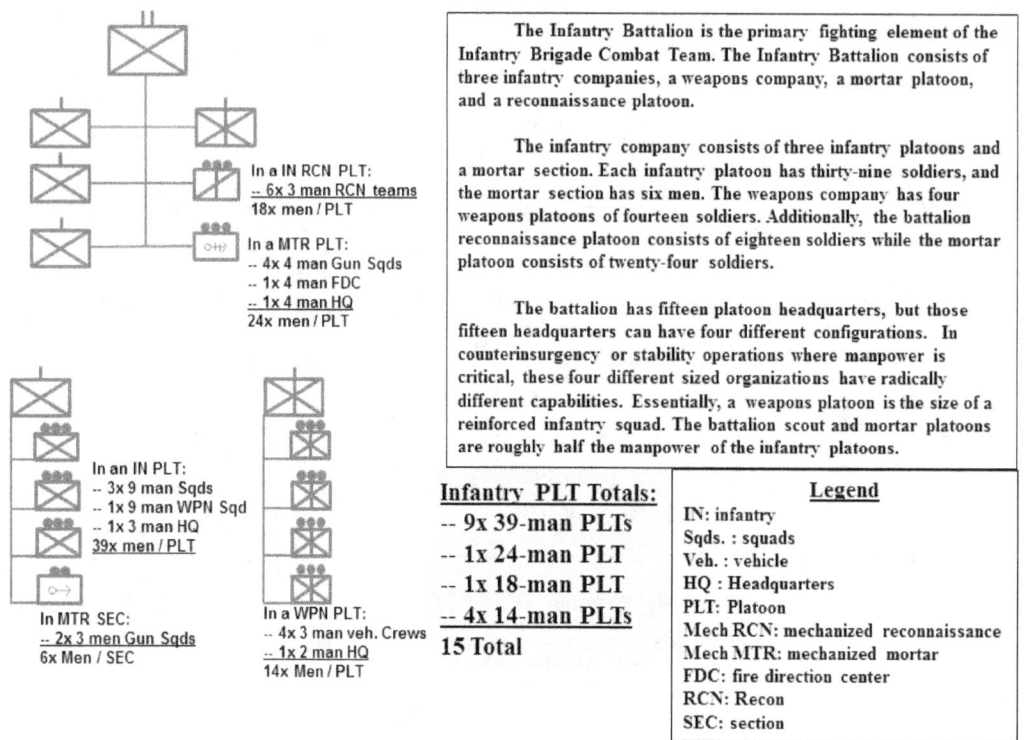

The Infantry Battalion is the primary fighting element of the Infantry Brigade Combat Team. The Infantry Battalion consists of three infantry companies, a weapons company, a mortar platoon, and a reconnaissance platoon.

The infantry company consists of three infantry platoons and a mortar section. Each infantry platoon has thirty-nine soldiers, and the mortar section has six men. The weapons company has four weapons platoons of fourteen soldiers. Additionally, the battalion reconnaissance platoon consists of eighteen soldiers while the mortar platoon consists of twenty-four soldiers.

The battalion has fifteen platoon headquarters, but those fifteen headquarters can have four different configurations. In counterinsurgency or stability operations where manpower is critical, these four different sized organizations have radically different capabilities. Essentially, a weapons platoon is the size of a reinforced infantry squad. The battalion scout and mortar platoons are roughly half the manpower of the infantry platoons.

In a IN RCN PLT:
-- 6x 3 man RCN teams
18x men / PLT

In a MTR PLT:
-- 4x 4 man Gun Sqds
-- 1x 4 man FDC
-- 1x 4 man HQ
24x men / PLT

In an IN PLT:
-- 3x 9 man Sqds
-- 1x 9 man WPN Sqd
-- 1x 3 man HQ
39x men / PLT

In MTR SEC:
-- 2x 3 men Gun Sqds
6x Men / SEC

In a WPN PLT:
-- 4x 3 man veh. Crews
-- 1x 2 man HQ
14x Men / PLT

Infantry PLT Totals:
-- 9x 39-man PLTs
-- 1x 24-man PLT
-- 1x 18-man PLT
-- 4x 14-man PLTs
15 Total

Legend
IN: infantry
Sqds. : squads
Veh. : vehicle
HQ : Headquarters
PLT: Platoon
Mech RCN: mechanized reconnaissance
Mech MTR: mechanized mortar
FDC: fire direction center
RCN: Recon
SEC: section

Figure 16: Platoon organization of an Infantry Battalion.[127]

[127] Headquarters, Department of the Army. *Army Tactics, Techniques, and Procedures 3-21.90: Tactical Employment of Mortars.* (Washington, D.C.: Department of the Army, November 2002), 1-18; Headquarters, Department of the Army. *Field Manual 3-20.98: Reconnaissance and Scout Platoon.* (Washington, D.C.: Department of the Army, August 2009), 1-13; Headquarters, Department of the Army. *Field Manual 3-21.8: The Infantry Rifle Platoon and Squad.* (Washington, D.C.: Department of the Army, March 2007), 1-11 – 1-17; Headquarters, Department of the Army. *Field Manual 3-21.10: The Infantry Rifle Company.* (Washington, D.C.: Department of the Army, July 2006), 1-11; Headquarters, Department of the Army. *Field Manual 3-21.20: The Infantry Battalion.* (Washington, D.C.: Department of the Army, December 2006), 1-3; Headquarters, Department of the Army. *Field Manual 3-90.6: Brigade Combat Team.* (Washington, D.C.: Department of the Army, September 2010), 1-10 – 1-12.

Combined Arms Battalion

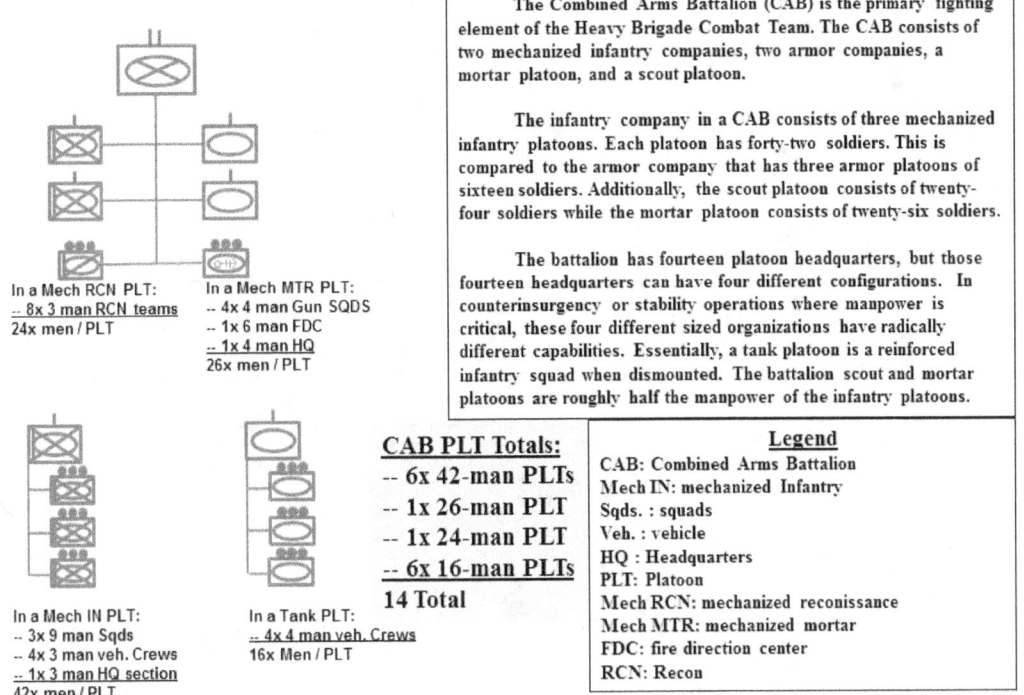

The Combined Arms Battalion (CAB) is the primary fighting element of the Heavy Brigade Combat Team. The CAB consists of two mechanized infantry companies, two armor companies, a mortar platoon, and a scout platoon.

The infantry company in a CAB consists of three mechanized infantry platoons. Each platoon has forty-two soldiers. This is compared to the armor company that has three armor platoons of sixteen soldiers. Additionally, the scout platoon consists of twenty-four soldiers while the mortar platoon consists of twenty-six soldiers.

The battalion has fourteen platoon headquarters, but those fourteen headquarters can have four different configurations. In counterinsurgency or stability operations where manpower is critical, these four different sized organizations have radically different capabilities. Essentially, a tank platoon is a reinforced infantry squad when dismounted. The battalion scout and mortar platoons are roughly half the manpower of the infantry platoons.

In a Mech RCN PLT:
-- 8x 3 man RCN teams
24x men / PLT

In a Mech MTR PLT:
-- 4x 4 man Gun SQDS
-- 1x 6 man FDC
-- 1x 4 man HQ
26x men / PLT

In a Mech IN PLT:
-- 3x 9 man Sqds
-- 4x 3 man veh. Crews
-- 1x 3 man HQ section
42x men / PLT

In a Tank PLT:
-- 4x 4 man veh. Crews
16x Men / PLT

CAB PLT Totals:
-- **6x 42-man PLTs**
-- **1x 26-man PLT**
-- **1x 24-man PLT**
-- **6x 16-man PLTs**
14 Total

Legend
CAB: Combined Arms Battalion
Mech IN: mechanized Infantry
Sqds. : squads
Veh. : vehicle
HQ : Headquarters
PLT: Platoon
Mech RCN: mechanized reconissance
Mech MTR: mechanized mortar
FDC: fire direction center
RCN: Recon

Figure 17: Platoon organization of a Combined Arms Battalion.[128]

[128] Headquarters, Department of the Army. *Army Tactics, Techniques, and Procedures 3-21.71: Mechanized Infantry Platoon and Squad (Bradley)*. (Washington, D.C.: Department of the Army, November 2010), 1-6; Headquarters, Department of the Army. *Army Tactics, Techniques, and Procedures 3-21.90: Tactical Employment of Mortars*. (Washington, D.C.: Department of the Army, November 2002), 1-14; Headquarters, Department of the Army. *Field Manual 3-20.15:Tank Platoon*. (Washington, D.C.: Department of the Army, February 2007), 1-2; Headquarters, Department of the Army. *Field Manual 3-20.98: Reconnaissance and Scout Platoon*. (Washington, D.C.: Department of the Army, August 2009), 1-10; Headquarters, Department of the Army. *Field Manual 3-21.10: The Infantry Rifle Company*. (Washington, D.C.: Department of the Army, July 2006), 1-11; *Field Manual 3-90.6: Brigade Combat Team*. (Washington, D.C.: Department of the Army, September 2010) 1-7 – 1-9.

Stryker Infantry Battalion

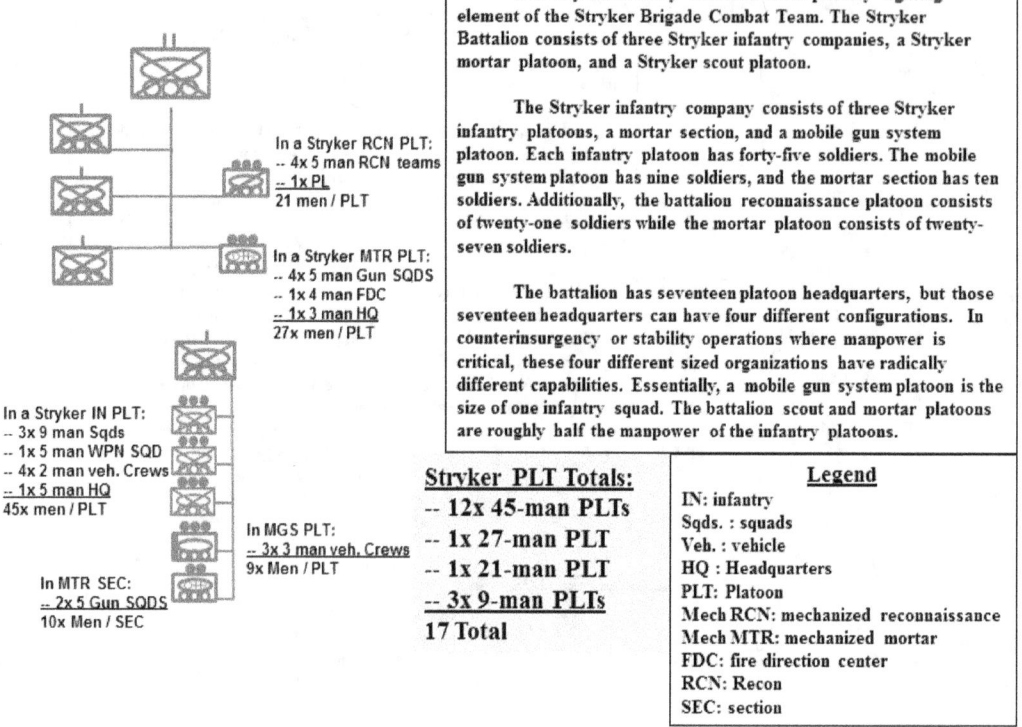

In a Stryker RCN PLT:
-- 4x 5 man RCN teams
-- 1x PL
21 men / PLT

In a Stryker MTR PLT:
-- 4x 5 man Gun SQDS
-- 1x 4 man FDC
-- 1x 3 man HQ
27x men / PLT

In a Stryker IN PLT:
-- 3x 9 man Sqds
-- 1x 5 man WPN SQD
-- 4x 2 man veh. Crews
-- 1x 5 man HQ
45x men / PLT

In MGS PLT:
-- 3x 3 man veh. Crews
9x Men / PLT

In MTR SEC:
-- 2x 5 Gun SQDS
10x Men / SEC

The Stryker Infantry Battalion is the primary fighting element of the Stryker Brigade Combat Team. The Stryker Battalion consists of three Stryker infantry companies, a Stryker mortar platoon, and a Stryker scout platoon.

The Stryker infantry company consists of three Stryker infantry platoons, a mortar section, and a mobile gun system platoon. Each infantry platoon has forty-five soldiers. The mobile gun system platoon has nine soldiers, and the mortar section has ten soldiers. Additionally, the battalion reconnaissance platoon consists of twenty-one soldiers while the mortar platoon consists of twenty-seven soldiers.

The battalion has seventeen platoon headquarters, but those seventeen headquarters can have four different configurations. In counterinsurgency or stability operations where manpower is critical, these four different sized organizations have radically different capabilities. Essentially, a mobile gun system platoon is the size of one infantry squad. The battalion scout and mortar platoons are roughly half the manpower of the infantry platoons.

Stryker PLT Totals:
-- 12x 45-man PLTs
-- 1x 27-man PLT
-- 1x 21-man PLT
-- 3x 9-man PLTs
17 Total

Legend
IN: infantry
Sqds. : squads
Veh. : vehicle
HQ : Headquarters
PLT: Platoon
Mech RCN: mechanized reconnaissance
Mech MTR: mechanized mortar
FDC: fire direction center
RCN: Recon
SEC: section

Figure 18: Platoon organization of a Stryker Infantry Battalion.[129]

[129] Headquarters, Department of the Army. *Army Tactics, Techniques, and Procedures 3-21.9: SBCT Infantry Rifle Platoon and Squad.* (Washington, D.C. : Department of the Army, December 2010), 1-8 – 1-12; Headquarters, Department of the Army. *Army Tactics, Techniques, and Procedures 3-21.90: Tactical Employment of Mortars.* (Washington, D.C.: Department of the Army, November 2002), 1-16; Headquarters, Department of the Army. *Field Manual 3-20.98: Reconnaissance and Scout Platoon.* (Washington, D.C.: Department of the Army, August 2009), 1-16; Headquarters, Department of the Army. *Field Manual 3-21.10: The Infantry Rifle Company.* (Washington, D.C.: Department of the Army, July 2006), 1-12; Headquarters, Department of the Army. *Field Manual 3-90.6: Brigade Combat Team.* (Washington, D.C.: Department of the Army, September 2010), 1-12 – 1-15.

BIBLIOGRAPHY

Abdollahian, Mark, et al., "A Formal Model of Stabilization and Reconstruction Operations." *Military Operations Research* 14, no. 3 (2009): 5-30.

Artelli, Michael J., et al. "A system Dynamics Model for Selected Elements Of Modern Conflict." *Military Operations Research* 14, no. 2 (2009): 51-74.

Artelli, Michael J. and Richard F. Deckro. "Modeling the Lanchester Laws with System Dynamics." *The Journal of Defense Modeling and Simulation: Applications, Methodology, and Technology* 5, no. 1 (2008). http://dms.sagepub.com/content/5/1/1.full.pdf+html (accessed on 16August 2011).

Barham, Brian D. "What is Relative About Combat Power." masters thesis, School for Advanced Military Studies, USACGSC, 1995.

Bumiller, Elisabeth, et al. "How Obama Came to Plan for 'Surge' in Afghanistan." *The New York Times,* December 9, 2009. http://www.nytimes.com/2009/12/06/world/asia/06reconstruct.html?pagewanted=all (accessed on 25 October 2011).

Box, George E. P. and Norman Richard Draper. *Empirical Model-Building and Response Surfaces,* New York: Wiley, 1987.

Campbell, Scott C. "Fixed-Wing Air Support Planning Models For The Brigade Combat Team." masters thesis, U.S. Army Command and General Staff College, USACGSC, 2009.

Center for Army Analysis, "Irregular Warfare." Database 2011.

Ciano, Joseph F. "The Quantified Judgement Model and Historic Ground Combat." masters thesis, Naval Postgraduate School, 1988.

Clausewitz, Carl von. *On War.* Edited and Translated by Michael Howard and Peter Paret. Princeton: Princeton University Press, 1976.

Cosmas, Graham A. *MACV: The Joint Command in the Years of Escalation, 1962-1967.* Washington, D.C.: Center for Military History, 2006.

Donnelly, Thomas and Tim Sullivan. "McChrystal Lite." *Weekly Standard,* November 9, 2009.

Downes, Patrick and Michael J. Kwinn Jr. "Proving Situational Awareness Impact in the Land Warrior Project" *Military Operations Research* 14, no. 4 (2009): 47-59.

Epstein, Joshua M. "The 3:1 Rule, the Adaptive Dynamic Model, and the Future of Security Studies." *International Security* 13, no. 4 (1989): 90-127. http://www.jstor.org/stable/2538781 (accessed on 16 August 2011).

Epstein, Joshua M. *The Calculus of Conventional War: Dynamic Analysis without Lanchester Theory.* Washington D.C.: The Brookings Institution, 1985.

Gallagher, Mark A., Gregory J. Ehlers, and Wesley O. True. "Defining Effects for Probabilistic Modeling." *Military Operations Research* 13, no. 4 (2008): 5-18.

Gentile, Gian P. "Let's Build an Army to Win All Wars." *Joint Force Quarterly* 52, (1st Quarter 2009): 27-33.

Goode, Steven J. "A Historical Basis for Force Requirements in Counterinsurgency." *Parameters* (Winter 2009-10): 45-57.

Gregor, William J. "Military Planning Systems and Stability Operations." *PRISM* 1, no 3 (June 2010): 99-114.

Hart, B.H. Liddell. *Strategy*, 2nd ed. New York: New American Library, 1974.

Headquarters, Department of the Army. *Army Doctrine Publication 3-0: Unified Land Operations*. Washington, D.C.: Department of the Army, October 2011.

Headquarters, Department of the Army. *Army Tactics, Techniques, and Procedures 3-21.71: Mechanized Infantry Platoon and Squad (Bradley)*. Washington, D.C.: Department of the Army, November 2010.

Headquarters, Department of the Army. *Army Tactics, Techniques, and Procedures 3-21.9: SBCT Infantry Rifle Platoon and Squad*. Washington, D.C. : Department of the Army, December 2010.

Headquarters, Department of the Army. *Army Tactics, Techniques, and Procedures 3-21.90: Tactical Employment of Mortars*. Washington, D.C.: Department of the Army, November 2002.

Headquarters, Department of the Army. *Field Manual 1-02:Operational Terms and Graphics*. Washington, D.C.: Department of the Army, September 2004.

Headquarters, Department of the Army. *Field Manual 2-01.3: Intelligence Preparation of the Battlefield*. Washington, D.C.: Department of the Army, October 2009.

Headquarters, Department of the Army. *Field Manual 3-0: Operations*. Washington, D.C.: Department of the Army, February 2008.

Headquarters, Department of the Army. *Field Manual 3-0: Operations*. Washington, D.C.: Department of the Army, February 2011.

Headquarters, Department of the Army. *Field Manual 3-07: Stability Operations*. Washington, D.C.: Department of the Army, October 2008.

Headquarters, Department of the Army. *Field Manual 3-20.15:Tank Platoon*. Washington, D.C.: Department of the Army, February 2007.

Headquarters, Department of the Army. *Field Manual 3-20.98: Reconnaissance and Scout Platoon*. Washington, D.C.: Department of the Army, August 2009.

Headquarters, Department of the Army. *Field Manual 3-21.8: The Infantry Rifle Platoon and Squad*. Washington, D.C.: Department of the Army, March 2007.

Headquarters, Department of the Army. *Field Manual 3-21.10: The Infantry Rifle Company*. Washington, D.C.: Department of the Army, July 2006.

Headquarters, Department of the Army. *Field Manual 3-21.20: The Infantry Battalion*. Washington, D.C.: Department of the Army, December 2006.

Headquarters, Department of the Army. *Field Manual 3-24: Counterinsurgency*. Washington, D.C.: Department of the Army, December 2006.

Headquarters, Department of the Army. *Field Manual 3-24.2: Tactics in Counterinsurgency*. Washington, D.C.: Department of the Army, March 2009.

Headquarters, Department of the Army. *Field Manual 3-90.6: Brigade Combat Team*. Washington, D.C.: Department of the Army, September 2010.

Headquarters, Department of the Army. *Field Manual 5-0: Army Planning and Orders Production*. Washington, D.C.: Department of the Army, January 2005.

Headquarters, Department of the Army. *Field Manual 5-0: The Operations Process.* Washington, D.C.: Department of the Army, 2008.

Headquarters, Department of the Army. *Field Manual 5-0: The Operations Process.* Washington, D.C.: Department of the Army, March 2010.

Headquarters, Department of the Army. *Field Manual 5-0: The Operations Process.* Washington, D.C.: Department of the Army, March 2011.

Headquarters, Department of the Army. *Field Manual 34-130: Intelligence Preparation of the Battlefield.* Washington, D.C.: Department of the Army, 1994.

Headquarter, Department of the Army. *Field Manual 100-5: Operations.* Washington, D.C.: Department of the Army, July 1976.

Headquarters, Department of the Army. *Field Manual 100-61:Armor and Mechanized Based Opposing Force Operational Art.* Washington, D.C.: Department of the Army, 1998.

Headquarters, Department of the Army. *Field Manual 101-5: Staff Organization and Operations.* Washington, D.C.: Department of the Army, May 1997.

Hoffman, Hugh F. T. "Making the Most of What We Have – Combat Power and the Bradley dismounted Infantryman." masters thesis, School for Advanced Military Studies, USACGSC, 1990.

Homer-Dixon, Thomas F. "A Common Misapplication of the Lanchester Square Law: A Research Note." *International Security* 12, no. 1 (1987): 135-139. http://www.jstor.org/stable/2538919 (accessed on 16 August 2011).

Institute for Defense Analysis. "Force Sizing for Stability Operations." R. Royce Kneece Jr., et al. IDA Paper P-4556, (March 2010). http://dodreports.com/pdf/ada520942.pdf (accessed on 06 October 2011).

Institute for the Study of Labor. "On the Production of Victory: Empirical Determinants of Battlefield Success in Modern War." Ralph Rotte and Christoph M. Schmidt. IZA DP No. 491, (2002). http://anon-ftp.iza.org/dp491.pdf (accessed on 18 August 2011).

Institute for the Study of War. "Accelerating Combat Power in Afghanistan." James M. Dubik, December 2009, under "Afghanistan Project" and "Reports," http://www.understandingwar.org/files/AccelCombatPower.pdf (accessed on 10 August 2011).

Institute for the Study of War. "Afghanistan Force Requirements." Frederick W. Kagan and Kimberly Kagan. briefing slides. http://www.aei.org/docLib/20090921-Kagan-Afghanistan.pdf (accessed on 7 October 2011).

International Security Assistance Force, Afghanistan. "Commander's Initial Assessment." August 30, 2009.

Kilcullen, David, *The Accidental Guerilla:Fighting Small Wars in the Midst of a Big One.* New York: Oxford University Press, 2009.

Krondak, William J., et al. "Unit Combat Power (and Beyond)." paper presented at the annual meeting of the International Symposium on Military Operational Research (ISMOR), Cranfield, UK, August 2007. http://ismor.cds.cranfield.ac.uk/ISMOR/2008/KrondackCunninghametal.pdf (accessed on 17 August 2011).

Krondak, William J., et al., "Unit Combat Power (and Beyond)." briefing slides presented at the annual meeting of the International Symposium on Military Operational Research (ISMOR), Cranfield, UK, August 2007. http://ismor.cds.cranfield.ac.uk/ISMOR/2007/cunningham.pdf (accessed on 17 August 2011).

Lanchester, Frederick William. *Aircraft in Warfare: The Dawn of the Fourth Arm.* London: Constable and CO., 1916.

Lepingwell, John W. R. "The Laws of Combat? Lanchester Reexamined." *International Security* 12, no. 1 (1987): 89-134. http://www.jstor.org/stable/2538918 (accessed on 16 August 2011).

Mako, William P. *U.S. Ground Forces and the Defense of Central Europe.* Washington, D.C.: The Brookings Institution, 1983.

McMaster, H. R. "On War: Lessons to be Learned." *Survival* 50, no. 1 (2008): 19-30. http://www.tandfonline.com/doi/pdf/10.1080/00396330801899439 (accessed on 05 September 2011).

McGrath, John J. *Boots on the Ground: Troop Density in Contingency Operations.* Fort Leavenworth, KS : Combat Studies Institute Press, 2006.

Mearsheimer, John J. "Assessing the Conventional Balance: The 3:1 Rule and Its Critics." *International Security* 13, no. 4 (1989): 54-89. http://www.jstor.org/stable/2538780 (accessed on 16 August 2011).

Metz, Thomas F., et al. "Massing Effects in the Information Domain: A Case Study in Aggressive Information Operations." *Military Review* (May – June 2006): 2-12. http://www.dtic.mil/cgi-bin/GetTRDoc?AD=ADA489043&Location=U2&doc=GetTRDoc.pdf (accessed on 16 August 2011)

Misak, Ronald E. "Capabilities-Based Planning: Maximizing Combat Power From Legacy to Objective Force." masters thesis, School for Advanced Military Studies, USACGSC, 2001.

Missile Defense Agency. "Mathematical and Heuristic Models of Combat with Examples." Jeffrey Strickland. briefing slides presented at the annual Interservice / Industry Training, Simulation, and Education Conference (2009). http://www.simulation-educators.com/uploads/2/7/7/2/2772366/907_notes_min.pdf (accessed 18 August 2011).

Office of The Secretary of Defense, Defense Advanced Research Projects Agency. "The Base of Sand Problem: A White Paper on the State of Military Combat Modeling." Paul K. Davis and Donald Blumenthal. N-3148-OSD/DARPA, 06 October 1992. http://www.dtic.mil/cgi-bin/GetTRDoc?AD=ADA255880&Location=U2&doc=GetTRDoc.pdf (accessed on 5 September 2011)

Office of the Secretary of Defense. Director of Net Assessment. "An Information Age Combat Model." Jeffrey R. Cares. Contract TPD-01-C-0023, 30 September 2004. http://www.dodccrp.org/events/9th_ICCRTS/CD/papers/166.pdf (accessed on 17 August 2011).

Olsen, Eric T. "Some of the Best Weapons for Counterinsurgents do not Shoot," *The Letort Papers,* Strategic Studies Institute: U.S. Army War College, 2010.

O'Neill, Barry. "How to Measure Military Worth (At Least in Theory)." YCISS Working Paper #7. York Center for International and Strategic Studies: York University, April 1991. http://www.yorku.ca/yciss/publications/WP07-O'Neill.pdf (accessed on 5 September 2011).

Operations Research Department. *Aggregated Combat Models.* Monterey CA: Naval Postgraduate School, 2000. http://faculty.nps.edu/awashburn/Washburnpu/aggregated.pdf (accessed on 18 August 2011).

Perry, Walter L. "Knowledge and Combat Outcomes." *Military Operations Research* 5, no. 1 (2000): 29-39.

Posen, Barry R. "Is NATO Decisively Outnumbered." *International Security* 12, no. 4 (1988): 186-202. http://www.jstor.org/stable/2539002 (accessed on 16 August 2011).

Quinlivan, James T. "Burden of Victory: The Painful Arithmetic of Stability Operations." *Rand Review* (Summer 2003). http://www.rand.org/publications/randreview/issues/summer2003/burden.html (accessed on 25 December 2011).

Quinlivan, James T. "Force Requirements in Stability Operations." *Parameters,* (Winter 1995): 59-69. http://www.carlisle.army.mil/usawc/Parameters/Articles/1995/quinliv.htm (accessed on 26 December 2011).

RAND Strategy Assessment Center. "Reflecting Soviet Thinking in the Structure of Combat Models and Data." Bruce Bennett. paper presented at the National Defense University's "Thinking Red" War Gaming Workshop (24 April 1985). http://www.rand.org/pubs/papers/2008/P7108.pdf (accessed on 17 August 2011).

Raymond, Allen D. "Assessing Combat Power: A Methodology for Tactical Battle Staffs." masters thesis, School for Advanced Military Studies, USACGSC, 1993.

Schmitt, Eric. "Pentagon Contradicts General on Iraq Occupation Force's Size." *New York Times* February 28, 2003. http://www.globalpolicy.org/component/content/article/167/35435.html (accessed on 25 October 2011).

Shirkey, Richard C. and Sean O'Brien. "Weather for Combat Models." *Military Operations Research* 14, no. 3 (2009): 91-104.

Schrader, Charles R. *History of Operations Research in the United States Army, vol II: 1961-1973.* Washington, D.C.: Department of the Army, 2008.

Swanson, Joel J. and John H. Gibson. "Combat Modeling for Command, Control and Communications: A Primer." masters thesis, Naval Postgraduate School, NPS, 1990.

Thiel, Joshua. "COIN Manpower Ratios: Debunking the 10 to 1 Ratio and Surges." *Small Wars Journal* (January 2011), http://smallwarsjournal.com/jrnl/art/coin-manpower-ratios-debunking-the-10-to-1-ratio-and-surges (accessed on 6 September 2011).

United States Army Command and General Staff College. *Student Text 100-3: Battle Book.* Fort Leavenworth, KS: USACGSC, 2000. http://elearndesign.org/tlacbeta/ikmeC105_norm1/15/xmedia/ST_100-3.pdf (accessed on 5 September 2011).

US Army Concepts Analysis Agency. "Analysis of Factors that have Influenced Outcomes of Battles and Wars: A Data Base of Battles and Engagements," vol 1 Main Report. Trevor

N. Dupuy (September 1984), B-I-3. http://www.dtic.mil/dtic/tr/fulltext/u2/b086797.pdf (accessed on 19 December 2011).

Walsh, John S. "Moral Factors: The 10th Principle of War." masters thesis, Naval War College, 2000.

Wass de Czege, Huba. "Understanding and Developing Combat Power." Monograph, School for Advanced Military Studies, USACGSC, 1984.